HOMOSEXUALITY AND HOPE

Homosexuality and Hope

A Psychologist Talks about Treatment and Change

Gerard van den Aardweg

SERVANT BOOKS
Ann Arbor, Michigan

Book design by Kathleen Schuetz

Available from Servant Publications, Box 8617,
Ann Arbor, Michigan 48107

This book has been adapted from the Dutch *Geaardheid of
Scheefgroei?*, Brugge, Tabor, 1984. Adaptation and translation
by G.J.M. van den Aardweg

ISBN 0-89283-265-7
Printed in the United States of America

85 86 87 88 89 10 9 8 7 6 5 4 3 2 1

Library of Congress Cataloging in Publication Data

Aardweg, G. J. M. van den, 1936-
    Homosexuality and hope.

    Adapted from: Geaardheid of scheefgroei?
    Bibliography: p.
    Includes index
    1. Homosexuality--Psychological aspects.
2. Psychotherapy. I. Geaardheid of
scheefgroei. II. Title. (DNLM: Homosexuality. WM 615
A768h)
RC558.A2   1985   616.85'834   85-2396
ISBN 0-89283-265-7

Contents

Introduction

by Paul C. Vitz

NO ASPECT OF THE CONTEMPORARY sexual revolution has been more talked about and caused more anguish than the issue of homosexuality. For years we have been bombarded from both sides of the issue. On the one hand is the extreme pro-homosexual movement with its cries for total tolerance and acceptance. The other extreme (more often underground these days) entails total rejection of the homosexual problem and an unwillingness to face it in any plausible way.

However, the most important issues involved in homo-sexuality have not really been dealt with. These are the issues of its cause and origin and the question of possible change in both homosexual behavior and in homosexual orientation. Today, after many years of rather strident controversy, there is evidence that we are finally willing to address these basic questions. In part this comes from a change in the public atmosphere surrounding the problem. The radical homo-sexual movement of the later sixties and seventies has now clearly begun to recede. Although the public at large has been awakened to the issue of homosexuality, it has also begun to back away from the extreme sympathy for the movement that characterized much of the public's reaction in the past.

Homosexuals themselves have begun to have second thoughts, have begun to reflect thoughtfully on the nature of their lives. The AIDS crisis has raised in no uncertain terms some of the consequences of a totally uninhibited and militant "gay" lifestyle. However, AIDS is part of a broader realization among homosexuals and others that the homosexual way of living, even quite independent of any medical consequences, has been very damaging for many.

In short, I think this is a time in American and Western culture when rational, critical, but sympathetic reflection on the homosexual issue is possible. Thus, Gerard van den Aardweg's *Homosexuality and Hope* could not have been published at a more appropriate time. The issue can be summarized as follows: On the one hand we have every reason to be sympathetic to and concerned with the homosexual, to recognize the legitimacy of his situation. He cannot be ignored, he cannot be simply ordered to change his behavior. Therefore, we have accepted the homosexual problem as a legitimate and important problem, one that needs to be addressed.

On the other hand, there have accumulated over the last few decades many studies relevant to the origin of homosexuality. Some provide strong evidence that homosexuality can be, and has been, changed. The early research literature supporting this view was once reasonably well known and accepted. However, as a consequence of the militant homosexual movement, this understanding has been pushed aside in the last ten or fifteen years and has remained a minority position within psychology. Dr. van den Aardweg shows that this research plus the more recent evidence is extremely important and insists that we address it. This, by itself, is an important accomplishment. In addition, he accepts that homosexuality is a serious problem but describes a psychological way for dealing with it. By doing this, Dr. van den Aardweg places homosexuality in a new context—namely, the context of hope for change.

Why should hope be so important? After all, many homosexuals seem to argue for the complete acceptance of their way of living as intrinsically valid. Here I think the evidence is clear. A large number of homosexuals are very unhappy with their way of living. When they learn they are homosexual, almost all homosexuals are appalled and depressed by this knowledge. The homosexual lifestyle breeds enormous amounts of guilt, not neurotic guilt (although I'm sure there's some of that, too), but true guilt: guilt over sexual promiscuity, guilt over constant lies about permanent loving relationships that are broken within weeks, sometimes within days or hours. This guilt plus dashed hopes about living a heterosexual life weigh heavily on many homosexuals. The hope that is being offered here is the hope for relief from these extremely painful behaviors, thoughts, and emotions.

A theoretical framework for change also gives us an overwhelmingly more rational way of understanding the problem of homosexuality and dealing with it. In recent years we have learned much about the many disturbing and debilitating psychological conditions that affect large numbers of people. We are now aware of the truly millions of people who suffer or have suffered from such conditions as alcoholism, compulsive gambling, drug abuse, manic-depressive disorders, schizophrenia, anorexia, bulimia, severe anxiety, depression, and phobias. Perhaps all of us, to some degree and at some time in our lives, will suffer from one of these conditions, just as all of us at some time or other will have physical problems.

More importantly we have grown accustomed to thinking about recovering from psychological pathologies—just as with physical illness. We all know people who cope with heart disease and high blood pressure, and who live for years with cancer. Great numbers of us know people who have recovered from alcoholism or psychological problems such as extreme depression and are the stronger for it. Perhaps we ourselves overcame such conditions.

Dr. van den Aardweg shows that homosexuality is one of the possible pathologies that all of us are subject to. It has its origins in the way we are raised and in various experiences of later life. As a pathology we can understand it—and recover from it. He takes homosexuality out of an extremely irrational framework and puts it in a rational and realistic context.

Homosexuality is not a permanent sentence, if you will, to a particular lifestyle that will always be antagonistic to the heterosexual way of life and to the major institutions of our society. Homosexuals are not condemned to a way of life that alienates, separates, and restricts a person greatly. Once we see and understand homosexuality as something like these other psychological problems from which one can recover, our perception changes in two ways. The homosexual is given hope for change and, at the same time, there is a kind of acceptance of the homosexual as part of normal, human society and, like the rest of us, subject to pathology. This is particularly true when we see homosexuality as a condition from which one can recover and in the process, God willing, become a stronger person for having successfully met the challenge. This needs to be emphasized. For example, I know of a group of homosexuals in New York City called "Courage." The members of this group are working hard at living a Christian life, in particular a sexually chaste life. They are well named—for to work seriously at such a way of living takes real courage. In the process of developing a Christian response to their homosexuality, these men are also becoming models of strength and courage for many others—including heterosexuals. For, in fact, many heterosexuals also suffer from pathological ways of living—in particular, various kinds of sexual behaviors common among heterosexuals are now recognized by many psychologists as addictions, such as sexual promiscuity, addictive masturbation, and sexual fetishism. Homosexuals who can transcend their condition will serve as models of strength and hope for many others.

In his writing van den Aardweg focuses on the experience of self-pity as central to the psychology of the homosexual. It is important to note that the neurotic consequences of self-pity are not restricted to homosexuality, by any means. That is, self-pity is a condition that cripples many types of people. One of van den Aardweg's major contributions is to describe the dynamic that gives rise to self-pity and some of the psychother-apeutic procedures that can reduce it. As such, his work here is valuable to people interested in the way self-pity afflicts the lives of people who are heterosexual as well.

Dr. van den Aardweg's use of humor as a therapy for treating neurotic self-pity also has application to many differ-ent types of people. Any person who suffers from the problem of self-pity is a candidate for the humor treatment. In fact, I think that humor is a very broadly usable tool in psycho-therapy, one that deserves far more theoretical emphasis than psychologists have given to it so far.

Dr. van den Aardweg's thesis bears upon a final major area of psychology—child-rearing and, in particular, the relation-ship of child-rearing to moral and ethical development. Certainly, the failure to develop normal gender identity has moral and ethical consequences. Dr. van den Aardweg very insightfully and succinctly describes the set of attitudes and values attendant upon failure to develop heterosexual orienta-tions in the child. His interpretation of the development of homosexuality provides a perspective on developmental psychology, in particular on the moral and ethical character of the child. I urge readers interested in that aspect of child development to pay special attention to the author's evidence and thesis.

Finally, Dr. van den Aardweg's approach is especially significant for the Christian community. He does not use any explicitly Christian concepts or theory in his interpretation of homosexuality or in his clinical response to it. Nevertheless, his book is a profound contribution to the Christian response to homosexuality.

The Christian pastor who had reason to think that homo-sexuality could not be changed was faced with a very serious moral dilemma. He could accept the person, but if a homo-sexual orientation could not be changed, he had to accept homosexual behavior as well. To do this, knowing that the Judaism of which Jesus was such a staunch representative unequivocally condemned homosexuality, was to reject the scripture and tradition of the church on this issue, not just for the last 2,000 years of Christianity, but for the previous 3,000 years of Jewish life as well.

The other option seemed in some respects equally unacceptable—namely, to reject the homosexual, tell him that what he was doing was wrong, but offer no help. Both alternatives seemed un-Christian, and there appeared to be no other.

We all know the famous story of Jesus and the adulterous woman in which Jesus refused to condemn the woman and wisely found a way to send away those who would condemn her. And yet, when the two of them were left, Jesus said in no uncertain terms, "Go and sin no more." There is real help in the present book as well as in the recent writings of other psychologists, both Christian and secular, who are coming to grips with the problem of homosexuality. They and Dr. van den Aardweg give important advice on how one can help the sinner who honestly wants to go and sin no more.

ONE

Current Social Attitudes toward Homosexuality

TODAY WE HEAR FROM ALL SIDES that homosexual feelings are normal, merely a question of preference or taste. A plea for social acceptance follows. Homosexual behavior and homosexual relationships are, it is said, equal to hetero-sexuality. As a consequence many urge, among other things, legal recognition of homosexual relations equivalent to mar-riage and more public "enlightenment" emphasizing its normality. The only problem posed by the existence of homosexuality, we are told, is social: making the public accept the condition and restore the natural rights of a long-suppressed minority. Some go even further and urge accep-tance for the idea that every adult is by nature partly homosexual; therefore, child-rearing should be modified into a more homophilia-friendly direction, by, for instance, iden-tical treatment for boys and girls.

In this respect the so-called homosexual liberation move-ment travels hand in hand with the feminist movement. Both agree on the need of an overall change in male and female roles and in the man-woman relationship. The watchword is that we must get rid of "prescribed" role patterns. "Prescribed" supposes that until now we were forced by the pressure of our culture into traditional forms of manliness and womanliness, into acceptance of arbitrary, imposed ways of relating to the opposite sex, and into acceptance of marriage as the only imaginable kind of sexual relationship. However, the argument goes, sexual nature is so much richer in its "variations," and modern science has demonstrated the existence of quite different, but equally natural, kinds of sexuality, sexual love, and sexual relationships. So clear the way for them, break out of obsolete prejudices! Anyone who cannot accept homosexuality as normal is accused of discriminating against people with a different endowment, people who are "inherently" different. Perhaps he discriminates because he himself is repressing the homosexual component of his own emotional life, or worse, because he is suffering from *homophobia,* pathological fear of homosexuality.

These ideas, constantly advocated on radio and television, in the newspapers and magazines, propagated by organizations for sexual reform as well as by established institutions in the mental health field, have left little room for other opinions. It has become customary to teach university and high school students that homosexuality is normal; a teacher who expresses a differing view might come under the pressure of public indignation. Authors of textbooks and journal articles in such fields as medicine and psychology regularly write with this mind-set. If opinions on homosexuality other than the doctrines of the homosexual liberation movement get publicity, they are commented upon condescendingly and with barely concealed irony. Small wonder that this is not the optimum climate to further unbiased research into the causes of this condition, let alone into the possibilities of its treatment, at our official scientific institutions. Most publishers hesitate to launch publications that do not join in the usual song out of fear of negative criticism.

One of the few who has berated the lack of freedom due to this social climate is A.D. De Groot, a Dutch professor of personality psychology. On the occasion of a discussion of the theory that homosexuals are more neurotic than heterosexuals, he wrote:

The most powerful Church of our time, among intellectuals and semi-intellectuals, is the community of followers of prevailing, trendy-progressive opinions. They accuse everyone who dares to put forward a theory of differences between groups of people of the sin of "discrimination."[1]

The propaganda for the acceptance of homosexuality has its main origin in the circles of militant homosexuals themselves. They are given a privileged opportunity to speak out whenever there is something to do with homosexuality in the media, or when an article, a book, or a movie on the subject comes out. Apparently, they are considered the best experts on their own emotional condition. On closer inspection, however, there is more reason to suppose that exactly these people "cannot be good judges in their own case," as the old adage has it.

Homophilia as an Emotional Disturbance

"Everybody says it is normal." I frequently hear this protest, mostly from young people affected with this problem. In the following section I shall explain why "everybody" is wide off the mark. Indeed, homosexually oriented people are often informed of their normality by medical doctors, psychologists, and even clergymen, with the addition: "Why trouble yourself about it? Accept that you are 'that way,' find yourself a friend, join a gay club. There is nothing you can do about it." Yet their opinions are unfounded, merely trendy thinking. Let us therefore propose an alternative approach.

To begin with, I shall show that homosexuality is an emotional disturbance that develops in childhood and adolescence. I shall then demonstrate that in many cases, those thus inclined can make a deep change for the better with patience, dedication, and good will.

It is not easy to strike the right note. As a rule, militant homosexuals shun an open discussion; they only want to hear that they are in the right. They turn a deaf ear to logical arguments and facts. They attack, dramatize their position, and, it is clear, they are highly successful in that. Their very militancy compels us to react firmly to their claims. But perhaps we had better pay attention to a not so vociferous and often forgotten group of well-meaning homosexuals. They feel troubled by their predicament and its consequences such as social isolation, remaining single, and loneliness. They often feel unhappy and inferior, even desperate. We had better pay attention to those who may lead a homosexual life but can find no peace with it, or who feel doomed to repeat, "I shall never be normal." Do not think this is a small group. When one inquires about it straightforwardly in a personal conversation, it appears that most people with this orientation are dissatisfied with it and would somehow like to change—"if only it were possible."[2] Certainly, many in this category resist viewing their feelings as *neurotic* or engaging themselves in actual attempts to change. We must admit, however, that their hesitations are at least in part reinforced by the prevailing social attitudes. In any case they—and all the more those who try to keep their homosexual feelings at an arm's length—are in need of realistic understanding, not overprotective or sentimental understanding. They need encouragement, but also rational insight into themselves. The following then is particularly directed to them, to their spouses if they are married homosexuals, and to their parents who (if not confused by "gay lib" propaganda) grieve over the course taken by their children's development. Furthermore, those confronted in their work or private life with the problems of colleagues or friends with homosexual feelings will find it useful.

TWO

When Is One a Homosexual?

T HE STATEMENTS "he is a homosexual," or "she is a lesbian," suggest that the persons concerned belong to a variant of the human species different from the heterosexual variant. Homosexuality is increasingly dubbed a "variation," a "preference," an "inherent condition." These terms suggest that one is born that way. This is a misconception, however. The knowledge we have at our disposal indicates that homosexually inclined persons are born with the same physical and psychological equipment as anyone else. It is no proof of an innately "different" nature, for example, that a certain percentage of men with homosexual feelings impress one as unmanly, even effeminate, in their behavior and interests. This is an effect of upbringing or of a learned view of themselves, a learned self-image. The "mannish" woman with lesbian feelings is not that way by natural disposition, but by habit and a specific inferiority complex. There are, on the other hand, distinctly "womanly," "feminine" lesbians whom few people would suspect of these feelings at first glance.

With the words "inferiority complex," I am already far ahead of my explanation. In fact, I will argue that homosexual feelings spring from a special type of inferiority complex: hence innately such a person is not homosexual, but heterosexual. This is irrespective of conscious feelings; a man or woman may have no, or only very weak, inclinations but still be in essence heterosexual. Strictly speaking, then, "homosexuals" or "homophiles" do not exist, any more than in the animal realm; you have only *persons with homosexual inclinations*. To bring this home, I shall mostly avoid the term "a homosexual" and use more cumbersome designations like "homosexually inclined people."

Homosexual Feelings

Homosexual feelings can be defined as any feelings of being enamored of, or erotically attracted by, persons of the same sex. This goes along with weak erotic interests in the opposite sex, or with a nearly total absence of them. We must make a restriction here: homosexual feelings during adolescence (puberty), up to about seventeen years of age, are usually transitory and must be looked at as a stage of psychosexual development. They disappear without leaving a trace when in the subsequent phase heterosexual feelings awaken. As I shall describe, puberty and prepuberty are the most important periods with respect to the coming into being of "genuine" homosexuality: homosexual feelings that survive throughout life.

Furthermore, we should keep in mind that the word "homosexuality" stands for a large variety of forms and types. For instance, there are men who feel aroused sexually by virtually every other man they meet, and others who are solely interested in specific types of males. In some, the homosexual feeling is continuously present in their imagination, like an obsession, while in others it appears more by fits and starts. Some are exclusively oriented to partners of about their own age, others to older ones, still others to young people, adolescents, or children (homosexual pedophiles). Some of them vary in their preference for a certain type of partner. Then there are differences in the roles they take on in the relation with their partners, some predominantly playing the active, others the passive part, while many—the majority—have no fixed role pattern. Some homosexually oriented people can at times be aware of clearly heterosexual feelings, of a somewhat reduced intensity, however: they are called *bisexuals*. On the other hand, some have only sporadic or hardly any heterosexual impulses, the so-called *exclusive homosexuals*. (I say "hardly any" because Freud rightly affirmed that in a careful analysis of the fantasy and dreamlife over the whole course of the life of a person with strong homosexual tendencies, one always finds traces of a normal, deeply hidden heterosexual disposition.)

Still another distinction: some cherish the wish for a partner for a lasting relationship, others could not even desire such a thing. Between the wish and its realization, however, these people find a great gulf; a really lasting and faithful relationship is extremely rare, if it ever happens. For example, in one study over 70 percent of the seventy homosexually inclined men and women who claimed to have accepted their feelings as normal and were living homosexually wished for a lasting relationship; but, by their own account, only four men and six women among them had had no more than one partner *during the two preceding years*.[1] No matter in what country or with what sample of homosexually inclined such inquiries are done, the results are invariably the same. It is nevertheless possible to distinguish between those who seek transitory contacts (the "cruising" types) and those who have affairs with one partner for a longer period of time—even if it is not that long.

Incidence

It is the militant homosexuals who gave the world the slogan that "one person in twenty" is a homosexual. This is pure propaganda. Some seem to think that a high incidence in the population would make the condition more normal, but of course there is no logic in that. Just because a high percentage of the population suffers from some kind of rheumatism, that does not mean that it is no longer a disease. If this contention were true, some tens of millions of Americans would be homosexuals. Such figures are not supported by research. The few valid studies—that after all have been conducted with selected groups—point to 2 or 3 percent of the population at most; one study did not even reach 1 percent.[2] Besides, take this into consideration: in all probability, fewer women than men have homosexual feelings (and most estimates are generalizations from male samples); 30 to 40 percent of the homosexually oriented are bisexuals and may thus be counted with the nonhomosexual part of the population as well; and children and adolescents should be excluded from the total number of homosexuals in the population, because their sexual development is not yet finished. That way, we come to even lower percentages and numbers.

It seems as if homosexuality has rapidly increased in the last years. I doubt this drastic increase; it may be only that the number of those who actually convert their feelings into homosexual behavior has risen. The overattention given to the subject (you can hardly open a popular paper without finding some comment on homosexuals and their problems) unquestionably contributes to the impression of the omnipresence of homosexuality. This is precisely the impression sought by advocates of the normality of the "gay" phenomenon. Being in favor of homosexuality has become a hallmark of a progressive vision of society.

Self-identification

Young persons who notice homosexual interests in themselves often go through a miserable time. They feel increasingly alienated from their age-mates because they are unable to share their interests in the opposite sex and they feel obliged to behave as if they do. They may feel ashamed; when the topic of homosexuality is touched upon, they want to hide lest others connect it with them. They suffer in silence; maybe they try to deny or play down their feelings, even to themselves. The moment comes, however, often around the age of eighteen, when the young person has to face his situation. Then he may conclude, "I am a homosexual."

That can give great relief. The acute tension declines, but a price must be paid. The youngsters hardly ever realize that they have fixed a rather definitive label on themselves with this "self-identification" and assigned themselves to a second-class and in fact excluded status. Some may take on a proud attitude and even pose as superior to ordinary mankind, but for all their show of being perfectly content with their "orientation" they inwardly realize that their "being different" is an inferior form of sexuality. It may be soothing to belong to a well-described minority and feel at home among similarly oriented people, free from the difficult need to keep up with the heterosexual world. The toll for this, however, is the depressing fatalism that is implicit in this newly acquired identity: "I am just that way." The young person does not think, "It is true that I have occasional or regular homosexual feelings, but basically I must have been born the same as anyone else." No, he feels he is a different and inferior creature, who carries a doom: he views himself as tragic.

This tragic self-labeling links up with an inferiority feeling that he has already nurtured for some time before, namely, the feeling of being a pitiful outsider. The idea that "I do not really belong" is now definitively stamped on his mind by the self-identification "I am a homosexual"—we shall come back to this later. The feeling of not belonging, of not being part of the group, with its consequence of keeping a deep inner reserve toward others, of keeping oneself aloof, is typical of most people with this problem.

Is that not rather the effect of social discrimination? No. It is true that the homosexually oriented are not really considered normal by the others, but the main cause of feeling tragically different lies within. These people retain this feeling when they live in an accepting environment. It is part of their neurosis.

Since many nowadays believe that you are just born with a homosexual preference which you had better accept, fatalistic self-labeling is more than ever furthered by the adolescent's outside world. Frequently youngsters who express their probably not-yet-fixated homoerotic feelings or fantasies are informed by the "experts" that they *are* homosexuals. That may hit hard and dash whatever hopes there were. I suggest as a preferable reaction to young people who disclose their secret feelings something like this: You may indeed feel that interest in your own sex, but it is still a question of immaturity. By nature, you are not that way. Your heterosexual nature has not yet awakened. What we have to discuss is a personality problem, your inferiority complex.

Sexual tensions can be quite intense, which makes the young person with homosexual feelings easily believe that engaging in a homosexual relationship will be the solution to all problems, including loneliness. He will, however, sooner or later come to the conclusion that he has landed in a completely disordered, in fact neurotic, way of life. His inner state will resemble addiction in more than one respect.

The homosexual style of life is represented in the media in a slanted, rose-colored way. That may be understandable as propaganda, but if one hears the life stories of practicing homosexuals over the course of many years, it becomes clear that happiness is not to be found in that way of life. Restlessness in their contacts, loneliness, jealousy, neurotic depressions, and proportionally many suicides (leaving aside venereal and other physical diseases): that is the other side of the coin that is not shown in the media. A minor illustration is the case of a famous German sexologist, who often publicly sang the praises of the enduring, faithful homosexual relationship, but who put an end to his life after a broken-off friendship, the last of many. His tragic death was hardly mentioned in the press—that might stir up unwanted doubts in some minds.

W. Aaron, a former homosexual, summarizes his many

observations on homosexual behavior as follows: in spite of the outward appearance, it ends in despair.[3] The American journalist Doris Hanson interviewed people who lived as homosexuals:

> "It's a rough world and I wouldn't wish it on my worse enemy," one man who comes through as an "addict" puts it. "Over the years I lived with a succession of roommates, some of whom I professed to love. They swore they loved me. But homosexual ties begin and end with sex. There is so little else to go on. After that first passionate fling, sex becomes less and less frequent. The partners become nervous. They want new thrills, new experiences. They begin to cheat on each other—secretly at first, then more obviously.... There are jealous rages and fights. Eventually you split and begin hustling around for a new lover."[4]

The mother of a young lesbian-feeling woman who had committed suicide told about her daughter:

> All her life Helen was looking for love. Then [with her last partner] she thought she had it, but the love was built on a lie. So it could never thrive.

Doris Hanson believes this mother recapitulates excellently what she herself had learned from her interviews. "It is indeed," she writes,

> A world in which emotions are built out of lies. To achieve momentary gratification from sex, homosexuals say "I love you" as often as they say good morning. Once the experience is over they are only too ready to say goodbye. The chase begins again.

I contend that these are not dark or moralistic exaggerations. The person with a homosexual drive is pulled to a neurotic and conflictuous existence. Stubbornly and imperviously, against all advice, despite the sorrow they inflict on their parents, young people with this problem cling to their "choice" of what their ignorance mistakes for "happiness." They do not want anything else—for the time being, at any rate. It may be hard, but it is true: not few of them degenerate, their youthful freshness and gladness disappear; they become weaklings in many respects—like addicts.

Fortunately, however, there are homosexually oriented men and women who want to take quite a different route.

THREE

Is Homosexuality "Inherent?"

I T IS AN OBSTINATE BELIEF that homosexuality is already "inherent" at birth. Most people do continue to consider it abnormal—contrary to what sex educators would have them think—yet believe one is born "that way."[1] To my knowledge, no reliable opinion polls among general practitioners are extant, but I suspect that a great many of them assume the existence of some inherited or some other physical cause. American psychiatrists, on the other hand, tend to view it as an arrest or blockage in the individual's psychosexual development and do not make much of physical or hereditary causes.[2] The impact of their opinion on the total scientific establishment is far from overwhelming, however. As a matter of fact, in 1973 the board of the American Psychiatric Association replaced the definition of homosexuality as a "disturbance" in its official Diagnostic Manual by the neutral term "condition." This occurred after intensive lobbying of militant homophile pressure groups.

One can understand that homosexually oriented persons often feel their drive as biologically rooted, for they experience it as if it were a strong instinct. Moreover, the awareness of being different was already present in their young years, although at that time it did not concern their sexuality.

Frequently they felt they behaved unlike their same-sex age-mates and had different interests and different likes and dislikes. They often felt like outsiders before the first homosexual inclinations presented themselves. Therefore, they came to believe that their nature must be a different one, that they belonged to some "third sex." In line with this is the tendency to glorify "being unlike others": some get the idea that their sexuality is the sign of a special emotional gift, seeing themselves as more sensitive or more artistic than the duller normal person. The inferiority feeling is converted into a delusion of superiority, but all on the basis of a belief in an inherited disposition. On closer analysis, the artistic interests of male homosexuals are rather explicable from upbringing and environmental factors. Some, for example, look for "soft" activities and interests out of a lack of daring and a consequent aversion toward "harder," more "manly" things. Feeling sensitive is typical of many neurotics; it has to do with a quickly hurt ego as we shall see below.

Both belief in hereditary cause and belief in other physical causes operating after birth lead to a pessimistic outlook on the possibility of changing. Homosexually oriented people who want to stay that way make the most of a presumed "biological basis." For instance, according to the members of an American "gay church," homosexuality is a God-created form of love. Would it not be permitted to live up to the Creator's principles?

The life of the theory of heredity is protracted as much as possible in the circles of militant homophile groups and their attendant liberals in spite of increasing evidence to the contrary. Time and again a single investigation or research report that would contain support for the normality idea is publicized. Studies on homosexuality must therefore be looked at with a sound critical sense, especially if coming from prohomosexual quarters. A recent example is the report of Bell and collaborators which we have already mentioned.[3] Their book suggests that a biological basis for homosexuality is highly probable, and among their conclusions they draw the moral that parents should rear their children "in accordance with nature." This means that children with a homosexual orientation need a specific (homophilia-friendly, of course) treatment, as if their presumed preference would be an accomplished fact from the start and clearly visible to their parents. Their work is a manipulation of public opinion; in fact, one of the authors is known for his prohomosexual stand. The statistics collected by the investigators are not concerned with biology at all, but with childhood, social, and other behavior of practicing homosexuals. From their material it appears that these people felt isolated from their playmates, which is an acceptable piece of evidence in itself, but which does not point to biology.

Fifteen years ago it was usual among sophisticated European homosexuals to quote the study of Schofield[4] as proof of the existence of a normal (and presumably innate) variant of homosexuality. His study did not bear on normality or abnormality, but on social and, more specifically, professional adaptation. He identified a subgroup of well-adapted homosexual men, which does not justify any conclusion as to normality or abnormality. In another example, a student of the problem finds no differences in the scores on some personality tests between homosexuals and heterosexuals. Predictably this is interpreted by some as evidence for the normality of the condition. However, if we check on what the test in fact measures—or pretends to measure—we find that it demonstrates that this factor is not directly related to psychological normality, or with whether this form of sexuality can be called a normal "variation."

Hormones

The terms "normal," "biologically rooted," "hereditary," "innate," and "physically caused" are often used interchangeably, although they are not logically equivalent. That homosexuality cannot be normal from a logical and biological point of view will be discussed later, but we shall first deal with the question of possible hereditary and nonhereditary physical causes.

Is it the hormones? many people wonder. No, according to an expert in the field like Perloff who wrote as far back as 1965: "It is purely psychological phenomenon . . . and cannot be changed by endocrine substances (hormones)."[5] This assertion still holds firm. It is true that occasionally a reduced concentration of male sex hormone (testosterone) has been found in the blood of men with a homosexual orientation in comparison with heterosexual men,[6] as well as deviant quantities of fats and metabolic products of adrenal hormones.[7] But such results must not be prematurely interpreted—as has been done—in support of the theory that derives homosexuality from hormonal peculiarities. Why not? Because this kind of difference in hormonal concentrations between homosexually oriented and heterosexually oriented men have not been found by other investigators. At least six studies in the 1972-1976 period can be enumerated that did not report abnormal hormonal values for homosexual groups.[8] The differences that sometimes are encountered are presumably connected with the specific characteristics of the groups under study and therefore not universally valid. They are sufficiently accounted for by simple explanations such as specific differences between the groups with differing sexual orientations in eating and drinking habits, in habits of living and working like being single or married, professional activities, or the use of muscles; and further by varied factors such as use of drugs or medicine, or differences in age.

In a group of homosexually oriented males, Evans found deviant values for metabolic products of adrenal hormones, fats, and a metabolic product associated with muscular development; further, deviant values for body weight and muscle strength, but not for sex hormones.[9] He toys with the idea that a factor he calls "reduced muscular development" has contributed to the development of a homosexual propensity. This study is one of a few that has come across something resembling a deviant physical factor specific to homosexual men. For that reason, we shall examine it a bit closer in order to see how results of this type are to be evaluated.

As with any scientific study, the study of Evans is not so interesting until his results have been repeated with other groups. Not before a series of comparable findings has been obtained in varying samples can a relation between that factor and the homosexual orientation be assumed. Let us suppose, for a moment, that a series of similar, mutual confirming results lies before us in the future. That is not at all likely; even if it were, it would not constitute a compelling argument in favor of a physical *cause*. The possible correlation between homosexuality and "muscle weakness" could mean, for instance, that boys with deficient muscular growth run a higher risk of becoming sexually deviant because of their feeling inferior on that account. That would be an example of the phenomenon of "organic inferiority" described by the well-known psychiatrist Alfred Adler. A child can develop feelings of inferiority because of any physical handicap or retardation, and as we shall see, it is precisely youthful inferiority feelings about the physical appearance, body build, and the like that can motivate a development to a homosexual orientation. Perhaps, however, our explanation of this theoretical case would be too far-fetched even in this form. Perhaps the phenomenon would merely mean that homosexually inclined males are less given to bodily movement of a certain kind, practice certain sports less, eat more, or consume more fat than with other men. An explanation like this one would hardly be startling, as it would be in line with the ways of life we indeed notice in many who are homosexually directed.

That the causes of homosexuality are not likely to be found in deviant sex hormones is, furthermore, apparent from the fact that individuals with hormonal deviations by functional disturbances of the gonads need not develop sexual abnormalities. For example, hermaphrodites (persons with the physical characteristics of both sexes caused by genetic deficiencies) who are biologically, i.e., genetically, females have an excess of the male sex hormone testosterone from the embryonic stage on, yet are not predestined to lesbianism.[10]

Everything then seems to indicate that sex hormones cannot be blamed. Now the hormones are eventually produced by order of the chromosomes; the sex hormones of homosexually oriented people thus point to normally functioning sex chromosomes.

Heredity

The sex chromosomes, extremely complex molecular structures containing hereditarily transferable information, can be examined directly in the laboratory. Homosexually oriented men and women appear to have normal male and female chromosomes respectively.[11] That is, we must assume that all organs and functions connected with sexuality, from the anatomy of the organs to the sexual brain centers—therefore the whole "infrastructure" of sexuality—are normal by heredity. The theory of an *innately deviant sexuality* or sexual preference therefore cannot be upheld.

Should one nevertheless prefer to hang on to a possible hereditary factor, such a factor would be only a *predisposing* one, a factor that would facilitate a homosexual development. It was a factor of this kind that Kallmann had in mind in 1958 for explaining the remarkable and interesting outcome of his research with identical and nonidentical (mono- and dizygotic) male homosexual twins.[12] He discovered that *all* monozygotic twin brothers of the homosexually inclined of his group had homosexual feelings too, although not to exactly the same degree. But only 12 percent of nonidentical (dizygotic) twin brothers of homosexually inclined men indicated no homosexual interests. The 100 percent similarity or concordance in homosexuality in the monozygotics, persons of a completely identical genetic makeup, is however by no means universal and must have been a consequence of Kallmann's specific sample. After him, a whole series of extensively examined identical pairs has been reported upon, of which one member was homosexually oriented and the other heterosexually.[13] Furthermore, there is a growing awareness that this type of twin research, however fascinating in itself, cannot decide if a property or variable of the personality is determined by heredity. Data like Kallmann's are explicable as readily by child-rearing and other environmental factors, or by psychological factors such as the high degree of mutual identification that is so striking in twins. That we should seek our explanation in that direction is clear from the rather high concordance in homosexuality found by Kallmann in his dizygotics (12 percent). This is a much greater similarity than the concordance in homosexuality between the homosexually inclined and their nontwin brothers. Dizygotics differ as much or as little in their genetic structure one from the other as any pair of nontwin brothers. In other words, the greater similarity as to homosexuality in dizygotics has nongenetic causes. For them too the explanation may be the relatively more intense mutual identification as compared with nontwin brothers, i.e., their feeling of being the other one's alter ego, and their being more equally treated and viewed by their environment.

There are some weak spots in Kallmann's study that need not be spun out here (a detailed discussion can be found elsewhere[14]). Here, I want to point out that the Kallmann data cannot be used as the groundwork for a genetic theory of homosexuality. Moreover, they do not even provide solid clues a predisposing factor.

Thus no genetic factor—sexual or otherwise—has been found that would differentiate persons with homosexual tendencies from others. Some investigators keep open the theoretical possibility of an as yet undiscovered genetic or hormonal factor for at least a subgroup of homosexually inclined. I surmise that they have in mind particular homosexual men who strongly impress as effeminate and lesbian women with strikingly mannish behavior. But not even they attribute a strong influence to that theoretical factor, as they affirm at the same time that the main causes are not in the hormones and the genes. Masters and Johnson take this postion.[15] These social scientists from the Kinsey school, although clearly manifesting their opinion that homosexual behavior is normal and fully acceptable, write the remarkable words:

> It is of *vital importance* that all professionals in the mental health field keep in mind that the homosexual man or woman is basically a man or a woman by genetic determination and homosexually oriented by *learned preference.*

Probably to avoid the accusation of being prejudiced, they hastily add that the heterosexual preference is no more a genetic given, either: an unreflective statement that can easily be refuted. Their lesson for "all professionals in the mental health field" about homosexuality as "learned behavior" however must not be forgotten even if we reject that wildly progressive gaffe on heterosexuality.

The history of the theory of an inborn homosexual nature— "inherentness"—is a long one. This theory has slowly crumbled, and now practically nothing is left of it. In his book *Changing Homosexuality in the Male* the psychiatrist L.J. Hatterer put it bluntly:

> Psychiatrists arrived at last at the conclusion that genetic, hereditary, constitutional, glandular or hormonal factors have no importance for the causation of homosexuality.[16]

No hereditarily transmitted homosexuality, no hormonal disturbance before birth or afterwards; neither deviations in body build, organs, brain, nervous system, or glands—it would go too far to include here the full enumeration of the relevant research reports; the general conclusions suffice. Until the moment that someone convincingly demonstrates that the homosexually affected person possesses some physical property, hereditary or not, which is not an effect of the condition, we can safely assume that he is biologically perfectly normal. As time goes on it seems, however, increasingly improbable that such a thing will occur.

"My grandfather was also a homosexual." "Two sons of my aunt are 'that way' too." We sometimes hear explanations like these from someone with this emotional problem. That does not mean that a hereditary cause was operative in their families, anymore than we could hold the genes responsible for the fact that someone's grandfather or cousin is also a Catholic or a socialist. If a homosexual orientation is of some frequency in families, we often see imbalances in these families in the role patterns of the sexes. Children are reared with underdeveloped gender roles, and they in their turn repeat this rearing practice with their own children. The women in such families may behave in a somewhat less womanly manner and bring up their daughters in a less feminine way, thus facilitating the development of inferiority complexes of the homosexual kind. They may have difficulty in accepting the sex roles in general, thus being unable to rear—and recognize—the boy as a boy, the girl as a girl. For the fathers, similar remarks apply. Otherwise, the relationship between family and homosexuality is very weak at most.[17]

Normality

Still another point must be made. Suppose a genetic or physical cause for homosexuality would indeed have been demonstrated, a hormonal peculiarity, for instance; that would however *not* have allowed us to infer that homosexuality is normal. Such a purely hypothetical factor would necessarily have to be identified as a factor of disturbance or illness. It would have been a *deviation* of the chromosomes or hormones, a *disturbance* of the normal physiological development, an infection, or whatever. It is good to be clearly aware of this, for one could easily think that to be born "that way" is tantamount to having a "natural" tendency.

Is Everyone Bisexual?

The notion of "inherent homosexuality" is invalid. May there, however, be some truth in the idea, which is popular with some psychologists and psychiatrists, that every human being has an inherited *bi*sexual disposition? In that case every man or woman would have equal chances of developing homosexually or heterosexually. The way an individual would go would depend on the child-rearing methods at home and, more broadly, on the influences of the total social environment in childhood. This opinion is espoused by Masters and Johnson,[18] and it was the opinion of the great Sigmund Freud himself. Nevertheless, the idea of universal bisexuality is implausible. As far as Freud was concerned, he supported his theory with now obsolete physiological material. Moreover, his concept was not completely unequivocal, a question that we shall let rest here.

If it were merely a question of child-rearing habits or of cultural customs that determine whether a young person would become homosexually or heterosexually oriented, or a fifty-fifty chance, God (nature, if one wishes) would have hung mankind's survival on thin thread. It would only have required a cultural trend in some early society to prefer homosexuality or to educate the children in this direction to bring mankind on the verge of extinction; and what trend is really impossible? Nowhere in nature do we see that propagation has been made dependent on such a gamble, that the survival of the species is regulated with so much carelessness.

In the animal world, genuine homosexuality as defined above does not occur. Animals may behave homosexually, but only out of lack of a heterosexual partner or by what might be called errors of perception and judgment. That is, animals can react sexually to specific properties of animals of their species: forms, colors, movements. In principle, these properties are attributes of the opposite sex, but they may also provoke a response if an animal perceives them in a member of his own sex, especially in the absence of a heterosexual partner. This is however not homosexuality in the strict sense.[19] Real homosexuality includes a lack of response to the sexual stimuli of the opposite sex. We repeat: is it likely that nature—or its Creator—would have been so sloppy with man, who is much more complicated and refined than any animal and obviously its most splendid product, as to leave, of all mechanisms, the one that sees to his survival, to the mercy of chance? Did nature forget to do with a man what she in fact did with animals: to establish a stable and time-proof heterosexual drive?

To pose this question is to answer it.

Otherwise, the bisexuality theory is contradicted by the facts. A. Karlen, a historian of sexuality, in his review of the incidence of homosexuality in other times and cultures than ours, writes that the most one can say is that homosexuality is treated in various cultures with varying degrees of tolerance, but that it has never been anywhere a desirable goal in itself.[20] Man has never felt an inclination to educate his children in the direction of homosexuality; the overwhelming majority in all cultures and times has been heterosexual. *By nature* man is attracted to the opposite sex. If it were not that way, then of the many peoples who lived at various times, there would have been exceptions, or at least one, to the rule that the majority are heterosexual.

The ancient Greeks? It seems that our imagination on this point needs some correction. Historians point out that Greek culture has always been heterosexual in its essence.[21] Homosexual behavior—or rather, so-called pederasty or love for young men and adolescents—was fashionable at a certain period and in certain circles, but definitely not the preferred or desirable sexual expression of the majority. Moreover, we perhaps had better take the picture of the sex habits of the

Greeks offered by a few authors of that time with a grain of salt. It is doubtful that we may generalize from the Greek poets, any more than we could get a reliable idea of the sex habits of our time by studying modern literature. What is eccentric and deviant is given a greater share in literature and art than would be justified on the basis of its occurrence in society.

That man would become heterosexual by child-rearing methods, repressing his equally strong homosexual component in the process, strikes one as artificial, especially when we realize how the heterosexual object choice usually comes about. It seems more accurate to say that development to heterosexuality proceeds automatically, instinctively. At a given moment, usually during adolescence, the attraction of the opposite sex is felt as irresistible, even by young people educated in a sexually restrictive climate, or without any sex education. It is also an indication of the hereditary basis of heterosexuality that one never sees young people who are free from emotional hang-ups, inferiority complexes, and inner frustrations, in other words, well-balanced, composed young people, who feel inwardly pushed to homosexuality. Nonneurotic young people are invariably heterosexual.

That heterosexuality is genetically determined is the inevitable conclusion. The brains of man and woman differ as a consequence of embryonic hormonal processes[22] and probably some of these brain structures constitute the biological basis for the profound psychological differences in the field of sexuality.[23] Some interesting arguments for the existence of innate heterosexuality can moreover be deduced from research into the sexual development of certain types of hermaphrodites, patients with sex-chromosome disturbances.[24]

A Transitory Bisexual Stage

We can, however, accept a special variant of the bisexuality theory, which implies that a teenager, during his development to biological and psychological maturity, goes through a stage when he may temporarily be erotically interested in persons of his own sex. At this stage, sexual development is half-completed and has not ripened to the full discovery of its goal, the opposite sex. It is in this phase of growth that various human and nonhuman objects and situations can be linked up in the imagination with the awakening erotic feelings that are still diffuse: children and older persons, but lifeless situations and emotionally arousing situations as well. The sexuality of a teenager in this developmental stage might be called bisexual, although there would be reason too to call it something like "multisexual." In homosexuals, the sexual development, along with a good part of the overall emotional development, has stopped at about this stage.

This is not to say that every teenager would clearly, or even feebly, experience the various possible kinds of erotic attractions at this age-phase. Perhaps no more than 30 percent of adolescents have at some time what might be considered homoerotic feelings. Erotic interests at this stage strongly depend on the whole of the adolescent's personality and emotionality, on his relationships with others, his social position, and his self-image. If homoerotic fantasies, interests, or practices develop, they are, moreover, usually superficial and tend to vanish quickly as soon as the physical attractions of the opposite sex catch the attention. In many cases, this discovery resembles an "Aha-experience."

Homoerotic impulses may go together in this diffuse stage with beginning heterosexual interests. In other cases, beginning heterosexual interests may be blocked by emerging homophile feelings, especially if the adolescent feels frustrated in his first heterosexual love affair.

Once the potentialities of the opposite sex having been fully discovered, the development is irreversible. Former "objects" become simply uninteresting—and this without a learning process imposed from the outer world, but motivated by the goal-directed and goal-seeking sex instinct itself.

FOUR

Homosexuality as a Psychological Disturbance

THE FIRST SYSTEMATIC STUDIES of homosexuality were conducted in the nineteenth century by such authors as
Krafft-Ebing and Magnus Hirschfeld. They interpreted their
data in the light of prevailing physiological and biological
theories of the time. The notion of the "third sex" or "inter-
sex," for example, became popular at this time. Sigmund
Freud pioneered the first homosexuality theories that stressed
the importance of psychological factors. He thought, among
other things, that the homosexually oriented person had as a
child overidentified with the parent of the opposite sex and
related in a conflictuous way with the same-sex parent.

Freud therefore went to childhood, and directed his attention especially to this parent-child relationship. He considered
homosexuality a largely psychological disturbance that was
probably spurred by as yet unknown biological factors (he
proposed heredity). One of the first nonbelievers in the
importance of a hereditary factor—perhaps the first—was
Freud's disciple Alfred Adler. This "discoverer" of the inferiority complex described homosexuality as the consequence of
such a complex as early as 1917.[1] His observations taught him

that persons with homosexual feelings invariably have inferiority feelings as to their manliness or womanliness.

Another disciple of Freud's who amassed impressive clinical experience with people with psychosexual problems and described some original observations on his homosexually oriented patients was Wilhelm Stekel.[2] Homosexuality, he theorized, is the consequence of fear of the opposite sex. Confirming Freud's ideas concerning the psychodynamic origin of homosexuality in childhood, Stekel minimized the importance of the supposed hereditary predisposition much more than Freud did and was perhaps the first to classify it as a neurosis. Moreover, he disagreed with Freud on the causal role of the famous "Oedipus complex" but indicated a number of failures in the upbringing of the child that could bring about the homosexual neurosis. He underlined the role of the father for the causation of male homosexuality, thinking it often more important than the role of the mother. He pointed to the infantile character of the inner life of these patients—he viewed homosexuality as a "psychic infantilism"[3]—and remarked that the homosexual motivation was intrinsically linked to feelings of unhappiness. More than Freud, he believed in the possibility of a radical change in the homosexual orientation, though he, too, thought that it would occur relatively rarely. His various observations deeply influenced the thinking of his pupils.

The second and third generations of psychoanalysts built on the foundations laid by their predecessors. An original element was introduced by the Austrian-American psychiatrist E. Bergler. He observed the so-called psychic masochism of the sufferer from this complex.[4] The homosexual urge contains, according to him, a kind of self-tormenting, an unconscious need to feel rejected and, in general, to "collect injustice," unpleasant situations, and experiences that give the opportunity to suffer (as it is said of some people that they "look for problems").

Another American psychiatrist, I. Bieber, and his collaborators have greatly stimulated the subsequent psychological research into homosexuality with their extensive statistical investigation of personality and childhood factors in male homosexuals.[5] I have already stressed the paucity of findings in the physiological and biological fields. On the other hand, Bieber as well as his successors have reported with clockwork regularity a number of more or less specific childhood factors in homosexually oriented men. These factors are intertwined and form a recognizable pattern that must be closely related to the process of causation. This pattern consists of interpersonal relationships with the parents, siblings, and the so-called peer group, as well as other developmental psychological data which it is not difficult to reconcile with the thinking of modern psychological theorists.[6] The statistics of Bieber and his followers can also be used as groundwork for the theory of homosexuality I shall present. They are the more acceptable for having been collected with varied subgroups of the homosexually inclined, and in various countries.

The present theory did not arise all of a sudden, but is the outcome of a gradual evolution of insights into neurosis and homosexuality acquired by psychoanalytically trained psychotherapists. Its founder, the Dutch psychiatrist Johan Leonard Arndt (1892-1965), integrated a wide variety of observations and insights of earlier theorists, notably those of Adler and of his own teacher, Stekel. Arndt confirmed and elaborated a number of Stekel's observations such as "He [the homosexual] is unhappy, feeling condemned to suffering by his fate," "I have never seen a healthy or a happy homosexual," or "[he is] an eternal child . . . who struggles with the adult."[7] With his introduction of the self-pity principle, Arndt did not cancel in any way the observations of his predecessors, but completed them into a synthesis which also accounts for other relevant observational data gathered by contemporary authors of various theoretical orientations. The homosexual, he said, like other neurotic people, may be possessed by an internal structure which behaves autonomously as the infantile ego, a child who is compelled to indulge in self-pity. Having discovered this mechanism first in some cases of neurosis not clearly sexual in expression,[8] he gradually became convinced of its occurrence in neurotic persons of any type, and finally recognized it in homosexuals as well.[9]

Arndt was impressed by chronic infantile complaining in the adult neurotic person, by its persistence and resistance to change. He used the current Freudian notion of "repression" to explain the fixation of children's reactions of grief and self-pity as well as their autonomous and repetitive character. For Freud, the important theoretical concept of repression was intimately linked to another essential notion—that of the unconscious.[10] Already in his first publications on hysteria, written in cooperation with Joseph Breuer,[11] Freud speculated that the intense emotions that may arise in reaction to frustrations are sometimes not normally worked through, but fiercely suppressed so that they become dissociated from conscious awareness. They retain their full emotional intensity, however, in the *un*conscious. Breuer and Freud especially pointed to the emotions of grief, with their accompanying manifestations of tears and sighs and anger.

Arndt identified the nuclear grief-reaction as self-pity. He theorized that this emotion had been repressed into the unconscious mind, thereafter forcing the neurotic to continually undergo the impulses of this self-pity without being aware of them as such. The therapy for this condition would logically consist of making the unconscious self-pity—the "inner complaining child"—conscious. Thus it would lose its compulsive power over the mind.

I initially adhered to Arndt's theory,[12] but my doubts about it increased over the years, and I finally rejected it. Undeniably, "repression" can account for several phenomena we regularly encounter in therapy. For example, we see the well-known phenomenon of *resistance* to admitting one's self-pity at the very moment it is at work. We may thus indeed say that something counteracts conscious recognition of self-pity. However, I think this "something" is largely equivalent to "hurt pride." Moreover, the process of outgrowing a neurosis, a homosexual neurosis for that matter, is best described as a combination of gaining self-insight and fighting one's recognized infantilisms on a broad front. It is not so much the unblocking of repressions that is responsible for the change as the gradual slackening of deeply ingrained infantile emotional habits, such as self-pity and associated reactions. The most impressive characteristic of the neurotic person is his self-centeredness, of which his self-pity is perhaps the most salient feature. Gaining emotional maturity largely amounts to diminishing this childish ego-centeredness and ego-importance.

I believe then that the neurotic repetitiveness and change-resistance are better understood as the effects of habit formation or "addiction" to self-pity and to tendencies intrinsically related to self-pity. Without deliberate effort on the part of the neurotic person to acquire self-knowledge and to combat his self-pity, the self-pity will tend to seek its satisfaction and thus to reinforce itself. Overcoming a neurosis is to break free from self-pity addiction. Freud's concepts of repression into the unconscious, and of the unconscious itself, seem to me too romantic. I agree with those who do not believe in the existence of the Freudian unconscious. Its existence has not been empirically proved.[13]

In the past decades, several other eminent psychotherapists have investigated homosexuality from a psychodynamic point of view; their observations and many of their theoretical conceptions are highly valuable contributions which are not refuted by the present theory. Some prominent names include Karen Horney,[14] H.S. Sullivan,[15] the French psychiatrist and neurologist Marcel Eck,[16] and the New York psychiatrists Charles Socarides[17] and Lawrence Hatterer.[18] Hatterer's book deserves special mention. He does not construct a general theory but rather describes a pragmatic procedure for the treatment of homosexual men. He describes many instances in his clients of such behavioral and emotional reactions as inferiority feelings, idolization of the homosexual partner, and the tendency to feel like a victim. These and other observations of phenomena encountered in the course of therapy are very worthwhile and fit in with the framework of the self-pity theory.

The proponents of the homosexuality-is-normal theory often contend that whoever continues believing that it is a *disturbed* condition, and more specifically, a *neurosis,* that is, a kind of *emotional* disturbance, is hopelessly backward. The idea that this disturbance can be overcome would be an even more serious expression of obsolete thinking. These proponents seem to be unaware that it is their own alternative that is behind the times. In effect, they always explicitly or implicitly resort to some "inherentness" theory, exactly the viewpoint of the nineteenth century. The insights in the emotional peculiarities of people with this problem, and the identification of it as a neurosis, are recent, as well as some methods of treatment.

Although the concept of neurosis is indispensable in clinical practice and there is a reasonable consensus about the diagnosis of a neurosis in individual cases, it has not been possible to find an objective diagnostic instrument for its measurement. Attempts with physiological and psychological "objective" tests for discriminating neurotics from nonneurotics have so far been unsuccessful.[19] Researchers must therefore rely on the one successful "subjective" test, the questionnaire, which, in the words of one leading researcher, "can be relied on to give excellent discrimination between normals and neurotics."[20] On a variety of tests, however, and in a variety of countries and socioeconomic groups, researchers have found the same result: homosexual groups consistently score higher on scales measuring neurosis than do controls.[21] This correlation is good scientific evidence for the neurotic character of homosexuality. These studies included groups in clinical situations—those who had already sought some form of psychotherapy—and those that were otherwise adjusted to life in society.[22]

In my opinion, anyone who tries to approach the available physiological and psychological research literature open-mindedly will have to admit that the best-fitting interpretation of homosexuality must be the idea of a neurotic variant. That relatively few social and other scientists of today seem to draw this conclusion, indeed that it is all but barred from publicity, is on account of the predominant prohomosexual liberal tendencies that censure unwelcome views. This is regrettable and paradoxical at the same time, as it is precisely during the last decades that a fatalist attitude about the changeability of homosexuality has become less justified than ever.

The present book is written after more than twenty years of study of homosexuality and after treating more than 225 homosexual men and about thirty lesbian women from the viewpoint of self-pity theory. In my opinion, the theory that homosexuality is a form of self-pitying neurosis is more than just a new synthesis of old material. It is a real improvement on former insights. Understanding the nature of this affliction is more than an academic exercise; it offers hope that those imprisoned by the prevailing dogma that homosexuality is inherent and unchangeable can be helped to become emotionally more mature.

FIVE

The Homosexual Inferiority Complex

A CHILD IS SELF-CENTERED by nature. His "ego" feels it is the most important, the central, being in the world. Therefore, he is primarily focused on himself. Put differently: he has a strong feeling of *ego-importance*. As a consequence of this self-centering, the child constantly compares himself with others (with the others as they really are, but particularly with the others as he sees them in his subjective conception of them). When the outcome of this self-comparison is negative, which it easily is, he will feel hurt: slighted, wronged, less loved, given less respect and appreciation than the real or imaginary others. If the child, with his great need of affection and appreciation, feels sufficiently appreciated, he is content, happy. He is likewise content if he feels privileged in comparison with others, or at any rate treated at least equally to them by men and by fate. However, as I have suggested, the child has a strong inclination to see himself as less privileged, less loved, in a less favorable position.

Just because he is so eager for appreciation, he is deeply disappointed by any real or imaginary lack of affection and appreciation. In that case, he has the feeling that his value as a person falls; he tends then to see himself as less valuable in comparison with others, possibly even as worth*less*.

The child's inborn ego-importance makes him overestimate the importance of incidental experiences of being less appreciated and also makes him overestimate the significance of "being" less valuable in partial aspects of his personality. Being "less" in some subordinate aspect of his personality or general life situation quickly becomes to him being inferior *on the whole*. For him, the idea or self-image of, for example, "being fat," "being less appreciated than my brother," "being a stammerer," "being the son of a socially humble father," or "being a failure at school" affects his total person. He then may feel inferior in every respect, as if the partial inferiority has spread over his whole personality. This is the reason that, as a rule, being appreciated in one area of the personality does not rule out an inferior self-image in another.

Feeling inferior implies thinking that the others cannot love you because of your lack of worth, that they do not really accept you, so that you do not really belong to them. Consequential emotional reactions are, among other things: shame, loneliness, self-depreciation, and naturally, sadness or anger.

Inferiority feelings can come about from comparison with others (the child himself is the prime originator of them, so to speak), and also from criticism coming from others, particularly from parents and other family members, secondarily by playmates and other significant persons outside the home such as teachers. In the course of time, when an inferiority feeling is reinforced by repetition of external or internal experiences that are perceived by the child (or the adolescent for that matter) as similar to the original ones, it can become chronic. It becomes a deep-seated conviction about the self (the "me"), something absolute, a negative self-image that starts living a life of its own. Once rooted, it proves resistant to new, modifying experiences and new learning. It is rigid and autonomous; all the affection and appreciation of the world do not seem capable of undoing it. This is why it is called an *inferiority complex*. To better understand this peculiar phenomenon we must dwell for a moment on an important emotion that develops in response to an inferiority complex and in fact is an essential part of it. This is the primal emotional reaction to a hurt ego of a child or of an adolescent: self-pity.

If a child (or adolescent) who came to feel inferior and to see himself as not appreciated or not belonging could accept his situation, his supposed lower importance, he surely would experience grief about the deprivation of love, the contempt, the deficiencies he noticed in himself, but by his accepting, the pain would decrease after a while. He would recover his inner balance and enjoyment of life. It is however difficult to imagine such a way of reacting in children or adolescents in view of their innate ego-importance. Self-relativizing is not an attribute of the child's mind.

The young ego must therefore neccessarily react with a self-centered emotion: he is seized by self-pity. "Oh, how pitiable I am! They do not love me, do not esteem me, they laugh at me, they don't want to accept me," and so on. And thinking about himself, that is, seeing himself in his own mind as a poor creature, he starts having intense pity for that suffering being. He feels self-pity in the same way as he would feel pity for other persons he sees as suffering and pitiable. Thus, "I am only ugly, unpopular, weak, a good-for-nothing, rejected, put at a disadvantage in comparison with my brother or sister" implies, "poor me."

Self-pity, as the word indicates, is pity directed towards the self. There is perhaps no experience or perception that can arouse a child's self-pity as effectively as the idea that "I am lonely," "I am less appreciated." Self-pity draws the ego's attention, its mental energy, more than ever to itself. The ego wants to comfort itself with his self-pity, which essentially is a kind of love: a kind of self-love. The child's ego wants to treat himself as a poor darling, as he would like to treat another whom he sees as pitiable. By means of self-pity, he provides himself with warmth, complains about himself, wants to protect and "fondle" himself, and feels entitled to comforting compensations. Self-pity expresses itself in words (complaining) and in inner complaints, tears, and sighs. It is apparent from a plaintive tone of a voice, from facial expressions, and from bodily postures. Self-pity nearly invariably engenders feelings of protest, whether in the form of anger, hostility, rebelliousness, or bitterness, because the child feels unjustly treated.

On closer inspection it becomes clear that what we commonly designate as an inferiority complex (following Adler's description), is identical with chronic self-pity for feeling inferior. I consider it to the credit of the Dutch psychoanalyst Johan Arndt to have demonstrated the functioning of the universal, and I would have to say, so very human emotion of self-pity. Every case of an inferiority complex is a case of chronic self-pity as well.[1] Without this self-pity, inferiority feelings would not have so many harmful consequences. Arndt called children's—and adolescents'—self-pity "self-dramatization," because the child feels and sees himself as an important, pitiable person: "My suffering is unique." His self-awareness becomes *poor-me* awareness.

The Complaining Child in the Adult

Expressions of self-pity (like weeping and complaining, and seeking comfort and compassion) can create relief and help digesting the experiences that caused the grief (the trauma). Yet children and teenagers who feel alone with their sad feelings for a longer period of time often do not unpack their soul in front of a trusted person. They are ashamed, or they believe there is nobody who could understand them. As a result, they continue feeding their self-pity inwardly. Children do not easily stop once they have started: this applies to many emotions and behaviors, as well as to a child's and an adolescent's self-pity. Once they feel sorry for themselves, they tend to persevere in it, even to cherish it, for self-pity has the sweet effect inherent in compassion and comfort. It can be very satisfying to see oneself as the poor, misunderstood, rejected, abandoned darling. In that respect there is something quite ambivalent about self-pity and self-dramatization.

Repeatedly fed self-pity in childhood and adolescence can generate a *self-pity addiction*. Put otherwise, it becomes an autonomous habit of inner complaining. This emotional state of the mind is described by the formula: "the complaining (self-pitying) child (adolescent) in the adult." The poor-me personality of the person's childhood (adolescence) survives in the same form; the whole child-personality is still there.

Thus we have three notions that for the most part overlap: inferiority complex, child-in-the-adult, and self-pity habit (also called "complaining sickness"). These are adequate descriptions of what is going on in the mind of neurotic people in general, that is, people with a variety of psychic hang-ups, obsessive emotions, inadequate feelings of insecurity, and inner conflicts.

The most important traits of the neurotic personality flow from the above formulas. First of all, we see the continuance of childlike and childish patterns. In a way, one can remain psychologically the child or adolescent of his past. This includes the child's specific sensitivities, wishes, strivings, and modes of thinking. Not everything of the child, however, is preserved in the adult with a complex. The maturation of the personality is seriously hampered only in those areas where childhood frustrations have operated, in other words, where self-pity and inferiority feelings originated. In other fields the person may have become psychologically grown up. In cases where the "complaining child" is strong—the complaining urge powerful—the personality as a whole strikes as immature, "infantile."

Homosexuality is just a kind of neurosis. The person with this complex harbors a specific "self-pitying child." This is why Bergler could observe: "In his fifties, he [the homosexually inclined man] is in his teens emotionally."[2]

A second neurotic trait is the usually manifest, but in other persons more concealed, tendency to complain, so penetratingly described by Arndt. The severe neurotic displays most conspicuously the urge to complain. He seems to be continuously seeking, and finding, reasons for self-pity and complaining; maybe he is chronically wronged, or always thwarted, or always suffering from something. His complaints can consist of everything negative: feelings of disappointment, being left alone, misunderstanding, lack of esteem, lack of love, any physical discomfort, pains and so on. It seems as if the neurotic mind cannot dispense with the feeling of self-pity, self-dramatization; hence one may view it as an addiction, or, what amounts to the same, as a compulsion to complain. As a result, the neurotic's normal self-confidence, trust, and enjoyment of life are damaged.

Another frequent neurotic trait is a childish desire for attention, approval, and sympathy, and often an excessive urge for self-affirmation. The inner child's longing for appreciation and warmth is unquenchable and as self-centered as that of a real child. In many ways this childish ego can try to be important, interesting, attractive for others, the center of attention in real life as well as in his imagination.

A final trait to be mentioned is the egocentric mindset. A quite large part of consciousness can be occupied by or focused on the infantile "poor me." To use a comparison: the "complaining child in the adult" cherishes and cares for himself as a pitying child would handle a doll she looks upon as a poor thing. Feelings of love for other people, having genuine interests in them, are blocked by the compulsive neurotic self-centeredness that has grown more or less spontaneously.

The Homosexual Inferiority Complex

Kinds of inferiority complexes and variants of the "inner complaining child" are legion. The homosexual inferiority complex is one of them. Hence, apart form the specific symptom of the homosexual desire, homophilia is not an isolated phenomenon but one of an endless series of neurotic problems.

We have noted that inferiority feelings may manifest themselves in several sections of a person's so-called personality sphere. The child or adolescent who is stirred by homoerotic fantasies and interests has inferiority feelings regarding his sexual identity or "gender identity"; in other words, about his being manly, or her being womanly. A boy then feels inferior *compared with other boys* as to his boyishness, toughness, sturdiness, sporting capacities, daring, strength, or manly appearance. A girl feels inferior *compared with other girls* as to her femininity in interests, behavior, or physique. Variation on this rule can occur, but the general line is unmistakable. Basic in this kind of inferiority feeling is the awareness of not really belonging to the men's or women's world, of not being *one of the boys (men)* or *one of the girls (women)*.

In the majority of cases this self-image of inferiority emerges in prepuberty and puberty between eight and sixteen years of age with a peak in the period from twelve to sixteen. In the later homosexually oriented adult this specific type of infantile or puerile self-pitying ego remains wholly alive, inclusive of its former fantasies and frustrations, its self-image of others.

Our point of departure has been an inferiority feeling, namely, the feeling of not belonging to the world of manhood and womanhood. Sometimes such feelings are fully conscious; the child might word them like the ten-year-old boy who more than once complained to his mother when he talked sadly about his contacts with the boys at school: "I'm just so weak!" (The mother told me this when she came to discuss her son's homosexuality.) Other young people can have the same feelings without their being clearly alive to them; they may realize them years afterwards. "Looking back now, I have always felt unadapted and not attractive compared to other girls," a lesbian woman pondered, "but I never quite realized it."

these gnawing inferiority feelings. Often they do not admit this suffering to themselves out of shame, for conscious recognition of your inferiorities can be a painful experience. It hurts your ego, your self-love or childlike ego-importance.

A child's or an adolescent's inferiority feelings can distort his image of the other persons, certain of whom may seem superior to him. In the boy's case, other boys and young men may seem more masculine or stronger. In the girl's case, other girls and certain women seem more feminine, more beautiful, more graceful, closer to the girl's feminine ideal. In that view the physical characteristics of the others may be central, but in other cases their demeanor and behavior. Members of the same sex, and some of them specifically, are thus *idealized,* even *idolized.*

A certain extent of idealization of same-sex persons is normal during preadolescence and adolescence. Boys of that age admire sportsmen, heroes, adventurers, pioneers: men with courage, strength, and social success. They feel attracted by domineering manly examples: masculine vigor and daring has a high status among them. They may therefore admire in general somewhat older boys, who are already "more of a man" than they are, and want to imitate them. Girls on their part pay special attention to the charming and womanly attributes of other girls and of women who already are more mature than they are. They admire easy feminine sociability, feminine grace.

Manliness and Womanliness: Cultural Stereotypes?

At this point we cannot avoid some parenthetical remarks on the trendy opinion that rejects the traditional ideas of masculinity and femininity and the corresponding "role patterns" as mere products of culture. According to this opinion, traditional culture has lived out its time, and therefore "indoctrination" of children with sex-role stereotypes is strongly discouraged. As a matter of fact, our explanation of homosexuality does not stand or fall with the answer to the question of whether or not patterns of masculinity and femininity are naturally given. Homosexual feelings, in fact, spring from feeling deficient in one's masculinity or femininity *as perceived by the child* (or adolescent), thus from comparison with others. Strictly speaking, therefore, it is not relevant if this masculinity (or femininity) is something relative, dependent on arbitrary cultural habits, or part of man's biological inheritance, or a mixture of both.

Nevertheless, the currently prevailing doctrine of fundamental psychological equivalence of the sexes can blur a sound judgment on gender-deviant behavior. Moreover, consequently egalitarian child-rearing practices seriously endanger a child's normal emotional development in general, and his sexual development in particular.

The equivalence theory is in fact untenable. In all cultures and times and everywhere in the world, men and women differ one from another as to several basic behavioral dimensions. The most plausible interpretation for this datum is heredity. Boys and men are, more than girls and women, hereditarily equipped with a drive to "social dominance," to exert authority in social life;[3] they are the "fighters" in the various senses of this word; and they are more object-directed in their way of thinking. Women on the other hand are more person-directed, react more strongly to emotional stimuli, and are emotionally more expressive. It is not merely a matter of traditional stereotyped learning that they are more caring and experience greater emotional "empathy." (Anyone who wants to delve deeper in this controversial subject can read May's resume of investigations into these gender differences with young children from various cultures, including our own, with adults, and with more highly developed primates that apparently have similar male-female differences.[4])

Therefore, the traditional role-ideals, now much reviled, of boys as "firm" and "strong" and "leading," the "conquerers of the world," and girls as primarily "caring" and "affectionate" contain more than a small grain of truth. That is not to say that one should exaggerate these psychological differences, nor that rigid and absolute behavioral rules could be derived from them concerning, for instance, the concrete occupations and professions that would fit the innate nature of men and women. But it does say that it is unnatural to assign the same social roles and other behavioral roles to boys and girls (men and women) when there are boys and girls (men and women) to fulfill them. And it does say that it is unnatural to behave as if different percentages of men and women in a number of professions and functions indicates "discrimination," social injustice. It also says that there should be made clear distinctions between the roles assigned to boys and girls in education. It cannot be wise, nor profitable for the society as a whole, to neglect the evident sex-linked preferences and talents for certain occupations and roles, and not to make use of the inherent sex-linked capacities and gifts.

The human psyche is profoundly male or female. This may be observed in children who are brought up with hardly any pressure in the direction of their natural gender roles. For example, boys reared rather like girls, by an overly present feminizing mother whom they identified with or imitated, or boys reared by older parents in an environment that did not encourage boyish behavior, nonetheless like boyish things in their hearts, even if their behavior is not so boyish. Often they will admire other boys they see as manly types. A girl reared with a somewhat contemptuous attitude toward things womanly and the female "role" ("sewing and all that sissy stuff, that's not for me!") nevertheless may be impressed by other girls and women who radiate femininity and inwardly admire them. More than once I have observed that women who lash out against this "oppressive feminine role" in fact feel inferior with respect to that very role. They in fact admire women who freely embrace their femininity.

We may look at it from still another point of view. Young men and women who are composed, happy, and free of inner conflicts do not ever seem to have role problems. They experience a determinate male or female orientation in several fields of life as something quite self-evident. Neither do they have troubles with the "traditional" man-woman relationship.

All things considered, the psychologically soundest philosophy is to take the basic behavioral sex differences as the starting point for working out the mutual relationships between man and woman within and outside of marriage. Dependent on time and circumstances, the concrete expressions of these relationships may somewhat vary, without leaving the pattern set out by nature. The sex roles are *complementary,* in accordance with the complementary nature of sex-linked gifts. Forced abolition of normal sex-linked behavior patterns, whether inspired by neurotic frustrations or by a mistaken egalitarian philosophy, will only put unproductive stresses on the relationships between sexes and serve the psychological actualization of nobody.

Homosexuality in Sexual Development

Man has a natural drive to identify with his gender. A boy wants to belong to the world of other boys and men, a girl to other girls and women. A longing for being recognized as one of the boys (or girls) is also inherent in boys and girls with inferiority feelings concerning their masculinity or femininity respectively.

As we have seen, a continuing feeling of inferiority generates self-pity and self-dramatization. The painful awareness of being different—in a negative sense—spurs a wish for recognition and appreciation from those idealized others, for *being one of them.* Eventually, this wish takes on the properties of a craving. This is understandable because it is based on a complaint of childlike intensity: "Poor me! I wish I were like them"; or "If only one of them would take notice of me, would care about me!" This sorrowful, self-pitying adolescent seeks *contact* above all: understanding, comfort, compassion, being cherished. Add to that, that he or she feels lonely and is frequently not an easy mixer, and it will become clear that the longing for an admired friend can develop great intensity. This mostly happens first in the adolescent's imagination. He may "fall in love" (in this peculiar way) with some age-mate, often with a young man who is somewhat older. It is usually love at a distance. The emotional undercurrent is, in any case, "It will never come true! I will never get his attention and love." It is a desire for warmth and appreciation propelled by self-pity, and this at the age when the still diffuse sexual drive is awakening. A pathetic need for warmth may then arouse erotic fantasies of intimacy with some admired friend. In other cases, the inclination to physical contact and physical nearness is not completely clear to the adolescent himself, although he may later realize that it had been dormant. Looking at other boys and young men in the street in a more than casual way is perhaps the most common sign of awakening homoerotic interests. He wants to touch and caress the objects of his admiration and to be caressed, to be near them, to be intimate with them, to feel their attention for him and their warmth. "Oh, if he would love me!" the boy yearns. The natural extension of this need of warmth and love is an erotic longing. This is not as strange as it might appear. At that particular phase of psychological development, preadolescence and the beginnings of adolescence, the sexual instinct finds itself in the initial stage of its unfolding, not having arrived at its final goal: the opposite sex. It is generally possible that a child, during this phase of gradual ripening of the sexual emotions, develops sentimental, erotically oriented feelings for a member of his own sex. This will happen more easily in the case of boys (or girls) who already feel excluded from the company of others or who feel lonely and inferior, longing for warmth. Their admiring interest in the physical appearance or personality characteristics of some others of their own sex then takes on an erotic dimension. The erotic daydreams or masturbation fantasies then become centered around the adored ones of the same sex—the homosexual wish comes into being.

In normal cases, a temporary interest in members of the same sex, more or less erotically colored, will pass by as the boy (or girl) grows up and discovers the much more attractive sexual aspects of the opposite sex. However, this interest acquires a special depth in the case of the self-pitying child who is overwhelmed by inferiority complaints concerning his own sexual identity. For such a child or adolescent, a bodily contact with some of the adored others becomes the fulfillment of the passionate longing for love and acceptance, the summit of happiness. Such a contact would remove, in the thoughts of the pathetic adolescent, all inner misery, inferiority, and loneliness. In this way, during adolescence, a coupling can be made between strivings for contact of a child who feels pitiable and eroticism.

The craving for a person of the same sex is passive, a quest for *being* cherished. It is not a happy and joyful experience like normal falling in love; the underlying feeling is of hopelessness, a kind of pain. This asking for love is of course entirely ego-directed. Homoerotic love is self-centered, "narcissistic."

Homoerotic feelings that come about more or less along the lines of the scheme described above can be quite weak at the outset but grow steadily more intense. The strengthening is often caused by increasing feelings of loneliness. Reinforcement of erotic fantasies at masturbation can considerably enhance them. At any rate, this erotically craving "self-pitying child" becomes an independent entity in the emotional life, what is called a "complex." The mind has become as it were *addicted* to this compound of self-pity and erotic craving.

Many homosexually inclined persons perceive their sexual drive as an obsession, chronic or temporary. Their sexual feelings often direct a great part of their attention, consume much of their thinking, more so than in heterosexuals. Homosexual impulses really have something compulsive about them, in that they resemble other neurotic disturbances such as phobias, obsessional worries, and obsessive-compulsive neuroses. They make the sufferer restless. The driving force of this compulsiveness is the dissatisfaction inherent in the inferiority complaint. This makes the longing insatiable, because the same complaint will always recur.

Nor can a homosexual affair or relationship satisfy or give any happiness other than a short-lived emotional "kick." The ideal giver of warmth exists only in the insatiable fantasy of the sufferer from this complex and therefore is never found. German sociologist Dannecker, a self-professed homosexual, incurred the ire of the homosexual movement by bluntly declaring the "faithful homosexual friendship" a myth. The myth, he went on cynically, may have its utility in accustoming society to the phenomenon of homosexuality—the lofty "durable friendship" sells easier—but by now we should accept the phenomenon in its full reality and have the masses accept it. This reality, he admits, is that we are after many partners by force of our "orientation." Dannecker corroborates his affirmation with statistics on the number of partners of the homosexually oriented as compared with heterosexuals.[5] What he says is not new. It confirms the compulsive character of homosexuality, its frenzy. It is not "gay" in the sense of "joyful"; it is an addiction.

An example of the inevitable course of events is the testimony of a homosexually oriented man who thought to have found at last, after years of "cruising" contacts, a genuinely loving friend for life. "At first I imagined I had really found myself in his company. I was sure that the unrest I had always had was caused by the need of a steady friend. However, the strange thing was that the same restlessness returned, and rather soon. Once again I saw myself confronted with the need to indulge in furtive contacts, despite my rather good relationship with my friend (for a couple of months)." The man's conclusion was that homophilia must indeed be a neurotic compulsion (he had not made up his mind, however, if he wanted to get rid of it).

We recapitulate: unconsciously, what the homosexual seeks is not to find and enjoy, but to ache and to suffer in order to feed the need for self-dramatization.

SIX

Origin and Functioning of the Homosexual Complex

S OME PEOPLE DEVELOP A COMPLEX of being slighted, others of being misunderstood, still others of being a failure, of being incompetent, of being not wanted, and so on. The inferiority self-image "I am only . . ." is invariably and inherently accompanied by self-pity, the "poor me" feeling. It is typical of the homosexual complex, that it concerns inferiority feelings in the field of one's gender identity. Why do some people develop a homosexual complex in their youth and others a nonsexual type of inferiority complex?

Origins in the Man

A boy can come to feel less boyish, less virile, when brought up in an overprotected, overanxious, meddling way by his mother, and when his father has been of too little importance in his education.[1] In the majority of cases the *combination* of such maternal and paternal child-rearing styles has predisposed to the development of the homosexual complex.

Before going on, we must pause for a short remark on the

question of guilt.[2] In assessing the parents' character faults and shortcomings in relation to their children, we may seem to point an accusing finger at them. That is not the case, however. First and foremost, our task is psychological and not moral, which means that we do no more than indicate determinate, observed relationships between parents and children, between parental behavior and subsequent behavior of their children. Secondly, personality shortcomings and weaknesses observed in a certain portion of parents of homosexually oriented people may not simply be imputed to them as guilt. These parents often act out of habit patterns of which they are hardly conscious, and they do not see clearly how some of their ways of treating a child can adversely affect it. Moreover, they are in part the products of their own childhood as well. I do not rule out their free will, and thus their moral responsibility. A certain measure of guilt is involved, since nobody can claim to be completely programmed by his education and youth circumstances. The extent of the parents' guilt cannot be evaluated, however, any more than the extent of the guilt of any parent as to his faults in rearing his children. The nature of our shortcomings as parents may differ, but all of us have our egocentric habits and other weaknesses, whether we are conscious of them or not. So while parents of homosexually inclined people may have their share of guilt, it will on the average be no more than other parents.

People with neurotic complaining tendencies sometimes maintain an attitude of reproach for what their parents have inflicted on them. One must realize that this may be yet another kind of complaining. Moreover, that prolonged complaining about the parents—of whom the complainer sees himself as the victim—is nearly always based on an unrealistic view of the parents. The complaining child's view of his parents is by definition a child's view, therefore one determined by ego-centered feelings. It needs correction if the person is to be more mature emotionally. Complaining homosexual neurotics may continue likewise to feel and to ventilate their complaints concerning their parents' wrong attitudes. This in fact feeds their "complaining child" and thereby the unresolved childish bonds they may have with their mothers or fathers, bonds of overattachment or bonds of aversion, as well.

For Christians, there is an additional reason why they should try to dispose of their persistent complaining about their parents' wrongs; they understand that they need to forgive. Some cases of homosexually oriented clients indeed show that therapeutic progress can be blocked by inability or unwillingness to forgive a parent.

Another effect of feeding childish complaints about the parents is that it inhibits assuming one's own responsibilities. In other words, the "complaining child" in the neurotic, claiming "I can't help it," does not accept responsibility for his behavior and inclinations.

Thus we raise the probability of the guilt of the homosexual neurotic himself. Is he responsible for his situation? Or is he entirely a victim of his illness, a patient? Our answer must avoid two extremes. The homosexual neurotic is like any other neurotic person, and any other man for that matter: not completely innocent. All human weaknesses and emotional habits of the average man—to which category the homosexually inclined does belong—have in part been formed by our giving in to them. This equally applies to self-pity, self-cherishing, habits of infantile self-affirmation and of proving one's importance, seeking attention, and so on. Some degree of guilt must be involved if a homosexually oriented person gives in too easily to his impulses, by masturbation or by seeking contacts, and even more if he justifies his behavior and recommends it. But that is all we can say about it. There is unquestionably much that is automatic in a neurotic complex for which the person cannot be held responsible, at any rate not to the full. This is true for any shortcoming of character and personality (we are not considering here people who are really mentally ill, such as schizophrenics).

Parental Relations

In 60 to 70 percent of the cases, the mother has been overly "binding" in one way or another: overconcerned, overprotecting, overanxious, domineering, meddling, or pampering. She often babied her son, or made him her favorite, her confidant. These influences have made the boy dependent, and weak, suffocated his spirit of enterprise, his courage and self-confidence. An overconcerned, overanxious mother transmits her fearful attitude to life to her son; a mother who wants to decide everything for him makes him will-less and without initiative. Boys reared that way display little of the normal, vital boyish mischievousness; they are overobedient or too inhibited.

It can also occur that a son becomes overattached to his mother by her immoderate—essentially self-centered—affection, her adoration; that places him in a special position. Then he is unlikely to part from her pampering and safe atmosphere and flees back to it as soon as the outside world does not respond pleasantly to him. Anyone who wants an example of the injurious effects of such sickly mother-son love should read about the life of French novelist Marcel Proust. He wrote love letters to his mother even as an adolescent, while they lived in the same house!

In certain cases, mother's love is at the same time compelling. For instance, mother threatens with hysterical fits if the son is not nice to her. In other cases, she imposes herself on her son in a more friendly way, but she is imposing all the same.

For all the attempts by defensive and militant homosexuals and liberal-minded sex reformers to play it down, it is an indisputable fact that their mothers occupied too central a place in the childhood emotional life of numerous homophile men. As a consequence, the son became overdependent on her, and he preserves this attitude toward his mother without modification in his inner "self-pitying child." This "child" will tend to transfer this attitude to other women as mother figures. Thus some have remained "mommy's nice little boy," while others continue behaving towards her as the "obedient, fearful little boy," "the dependent boy," and sometimes the "repressed, tyrannized boy." These mother-ties are unhealthy, a great inhibition to becoming an adult man.

After having a great many contacts with homosexually afflicted men in the course of his professional life, the investigator and therapist I. Bieber writes that in not one single case had there been a normal father-son relationship.[3] Mostly the father had been "detached," not involved in his son's everyday life and interests. My experience is much the same. A more detailed analysis of a variety of psychological childhood factors in a subgroup of 120 of my male clients with this problem yielded two or three cases at most where the father-son relationship could be considered good. Even in these cases the relationship with the father was distant. The father of one homosexually inclined man was already old when his son was a boy, and in another case the affective father-son tie seemed to me rather shallow. We are then correct to state that the father-son relationship is seldom positive. A man who develops a homosexual inferiority complex has generally found his father not enough of a father.

The deficient relationship with the father may have had several causes. A psychologically distant father sometimes pays little attention to his son because the latter was one of the younger siblings in a larger family. A father's interest may have concentrated on his older sons. In some cases, father regarded the boy as his wife's business; the existence of an exclusive mother-son tie may have conditioned this fatherly attitude.

A good example of such a situation was the Dutch novelist Louis Couperus, who lived at the beginning of this century. He developed an inferiority complex as to his "being a weakling." This self-image originated because he felt hurt by his father's lack of appreciation. The father left his youngest son Louis under the care of mother and of his older sisters and did not accept him in his own world, which he shared with the boys' older brothers.[4]

Some fathers were too busy to spend enough time with their family, and with one boy in particular. Another group of fathers were classic "weak personalities," not masculine enough themselves, too dependent, fearful, sometimes leaning too much on their wives. They were weak as models of virility so that their sons had a deficient model to identify with. Relatively old fathers lacked the youthful dynamism necessary for their boys' development. They did not romp with them or encourage boyish activities. As a result, their sons' behavior became prissy, like a "little old man."

In about a quarter of my cases and those of others, the son experienced his father as distinctly negative. His father criticized him, did not give him much approval, so that this son felt rejected by the principal man of his world. The boy may also have felt slighted by his father's comparing him to his brothers (and sisters). In a certain percentage of the cases—probably about 20 percent—the experience of rejection by his father even seems to have been the crucial factor of psycho-traumatization (injury), making the boy feel excluded from the men's world. For a boy, his father is the prototype of the man. Feeling appreciated by his father is essential to his self-confidence as a man. The same is true for the girl in relation to her mother.

Other Influences

On the average, the weight of the father factor seems to me to be greater than that of the mother factor. Chances of a homosexual development are, however, substantially enhanced if the influence of both factors are present. As a rule, male homosexuality results from the combined shortcomings of the parents.

In this connection we must note that in a good many of our cases, deep-seated problems existed between the client's parents. These problems were generally of the following sort: sometimes the mother was pronouncedly the "stronger," domineering personality of the two, forcing her husband to withdraw. Sometimes the mother suffered from her husband's neglect, and her dissatisfaction drew her closer to one of her sons. In general, a woman has a natural tendency to make one man in her environment "her man"; if she has no emotional tie with her husband she may seek a substitute in a bond with a son.

Many kinds of marital tensions can, of course, occur. They originate in a variety of egocentric habits and in the kind of still infantile ways of acting and reacting that we all take with us into married life. The incidence of satisfactory marriage relationships is, however, statistically lower among parents of the homosexually inclined than among parents whose children did not develop this complex. This helps us understand once again that homosexuality is not only a phenomenon of the one so concerned, but is also a symptom of imbalance in the family and not infrequently of parental discord.

Otherwise, the personalities of the parents, their relations one with another and with their children, and their child-rearing practices are not the only factors predisposing to homosexuality. Within the family, some of the following factors may contribute to such a development: position in the series of siblings, proportion of boys to girls, sibling rivalry, or teasing. For example, according to some studies, homosexually inclined men were, more often than heterosexuals, the younger boys of larger families. This suggests more over-protection on the part of the mother and perhaps also an older, more distant, father. Some men with this complex came from families in which boys predominated, a situation that may have provoked in the mother the tendency to treat one of her boys more like a girl. A boy might also be encouraged to develop this complex by looking upon himself as the weakest, least virile, of his brothers—as a result of his comparing himself with them, or of their teasing or ridiculing him. The "teasing" factor has been extremely important in a number of persons I have seen with this inferiority complex. Comparison with a particular brother who was viewed as more sturdy, more healthy, and the like, seems in other cases to have been the factor that tipped the balance in the wrong direction.

Finally, we must note the influence of predisposing factors like the self-image of being ugly and physically weak. A boy may have suffered for some time from the idea that he was flabby, sickly, asthmatic, too short, too thin, or too fat. These self-images were experienced as variants of being "unmanly," not strong or attractive as a male.

The result of the above parental and other factors can be a lack of boyishness in behavior and interests, more specifically, a lack of daring and self-confidence in boyish activities such as fighting. The boy runs away from those activities, saying "that is not for me." For instance, studies reveal that most of the men with this complex had an outspoken childhood aversion for soccer or other group games. Such games are more or less the embodiment of boyish activity in our culture; they require enjoying competition with other boys and some fighting spirit and indicate adjustment to the peer group.[5]

The next step in the development of the homosexual complex is decisive. It is the boy's *self-comparison with same-sex age-mates*. Should a boy with the unfavorable family influences we described still succeed in crossing the threshold to boyish activities and enter the boys' world—with the encouragement of others, for example—the danger of homosexual development would have been exorcised. Things often do not take that positive course, and instead of conquering for himself a position among the boys, the discouraged boy withdraws, a prey of feelings of insufficiency and self-pity. If he can make any friend, it is an outsider like himself; he feels lonely and apart. Not infrequently, such a boy is teased and ridiculed for his lack of daring, for being a "sissy," for being "old maidish," and the like.

Many went through an adolescent or preadolescent period

of loneliness and depression. Then comes the third step in the developmental process. The boy starts longing to be like the others and to have a friend who is like them. The homoerotic wish for compassion and comfort associates itself with the onset of self-dramatization.

Statistically, homosexuality is most closely tied to these "social adaptation" factors, or "peer" factors, even more so than to the factors concerning parents and family situations.[6] The inner drama of these men as children or adolescents was that they could not really feel part of the boyhood community.

Origins in the Woman

The situation of the girl who later feels homosexually attracted to other women is in more than one respect the mirror image of that of the boy. The comparison with a mirror image does not hold perfectly, though, since the pattern of preparing factors in the woman has often been more varied than in the man.[7]

As children, many women with lesbian feelings felt a lack of understanding on the part of their mother. This feeling of distance from the mother has several variants. For example, as one woman summarized it: "My mother did everything for me, but I could hardly talk with her about my personal and emotional things." Other complaints went: "My mother never had time for me," "My mother had much more contact with my sister than with me," "She arranged everything for me, and kept me a small child," "She was often ill," "She was institutionalized several times in a mental hospital," "She left the family when I was still young," and so on.

Sometimes, the girl had to assume the mother's role herself for her siblings—as the oldest girl, for instance, or in cases where mother did not function well as a mother—and this made her feel deprived of the warmth of an understanding mother herself.

The mother may have felt inhibited in her functioning as a

woman, or not felt at home in her female role. That inspired in her a critical attitude toward what she saw as the female role, for instance, and she transferred that attitude to her daughter. The girl thus developed an attitude that rejected her feminine side. Some lesbian women had the idea that their mother would have preferred a boy to them and therefore stimulated boyish behavior and achievements in them instead of those appropriate for a girl.

The girl's self-confidence as a woman is primarily formed by her mother. When a mother succeeds in making her daughter feel appreciated as a female, the girl will feel at home in the women's world and among her age-mates of the same sex. In homosexually oriented women, very often the relationship with mother was not a personal and confidential one; there was no sharing of womanly interests, no joint activities in the "female area." As a consequence, the girl did not feel valuable *as a girl*; that is, different from a boy, but just as valuable.

Considerable variation seems to occur in the patterns of father-daughter relations as well. Some women with lesbian feelings were excessively attached to their fathers, as "his special friend." Sometimes this attachment was more or less forced on them, as the father wanted them in a specific role, so that the relationship was not unconstrained and natural. The father sometimes would have preferred this daughter to have been a son, a comrade, and he stimulated in her certain male roles, interests, and achievements. He overemphasized, for example, her professional performance in school or her achievement in sports and her functioning in important social roles. Understandably, somewhere deep down the girl felt misunderstood and not genuinely accepted as the person she in fact was.

In other cases, the father sought in his daughter a helping, comforting mother figure. He had a praising attitude to her, placed her in a privileged position but in fact bought her dedication to him by this behavior. There have been also fathers with weak personalities who leaned too much on their wives. In all these cases, the emotional ties with the father are fixated in the adult lesbian woman's "inner child of the past."

Other women with this problem were not so much "daddy's girl," rather they were, or saw themselves as, the unwished for, the disapproved daughter. She was often criticized by him, felt his contempt, at least his lack of interest in her. Overcompensatory masculine behaviors and interests in some of these women can be accounted for as a reaction to this unaccepting paternal attitude. The girl then learned to see the masculine role as superior and tried to catch up with it. Again, negative feelings toward the father as well as the overcompensatory masculine strivings in order to live up to his standards and thus get his appreciation will live on in the neurotic complex. A good and normal father-daughter relationship, to conclude, is statistically less frequent in homosexually oriented women than in the heterosexually oriented.

Other Influences

In some women, an ugliness complex, with the emphasis on feeling less feminine, less attractive as a girl, may also have played a part as a precipitating factor. In other cases, it was the comparison with a sister who was considered (by the girl herself or by her environment) the better one in physical attractiveness or in other respects. In still other ones, the girl felt inferior among her brothers—"I am *only* a girl"—and on this basis tried to emulate them in boyishness. In adolescence, the attention given her by the opposite sex may have created her sensitive point: "They do not find me as attractive as other girls," "they do not date me," and so on. A girl who feels less appreciated by the boys may come to admire the woman-liness of other girls who are more sought after. Predisposing factors like the ones mentioned above usually operate together and are mutually reinforcing with girls as with boys.

A portion of the girls who later developed a lesbian complex indeed behaved in a somewhat less girlish or less ladylike way than their age-mates. That provoked them to feel insecure in the field of femininity, with possible overcompensatory reactions like taking on attitudes of carelessness and indifference, bossing and domineering, trying to outdo the boys in masculinity, daring everything, behaving aggressively, being rough and tough. They may have developed a manifest dislike for feminine behavior, clothes, and domestic activities. This overcompensatory mannish self-assertiveness is, however, marked by a lack of natural smoothness. It is overdone; the emotional tension underneath is perceptible.

This is not to say that all women with this complex tend to behave in a "mannish" way. Nor do women who assert themselves that way always need to have lesbian inclinations; but there is a correlation between these two traits. Overly mannish behavior in women, however, nearly always is a sign of an inferiority complex.

The main factor on the development of a lesbian orientation is a girl's self-comparison with same-sex age-mates or with certain older "ideal" women. As in the case of boys, the crucial factor is *subjective,* namely, the child's perception of herself. For this reason, sometimes, although not often, a girl whose behavior is objectively quite feminine can develop such a complex.

In adolescence a girl wishes to have girlfriends and to be one with them. Her loneliness and feeling of separation stir longings for admired girlfriends or ideal woman figures. If a girl feels slighted as to her mother's affection and understanding, she can turn to an ideal type of woman possessing in her eyes the desired motherly characteristics: for instance, an easygoing, affectionate teacher, or an older girl with motherly attitudes. The self-pitying girl wants the exclusive attention of her idol, clutches to her: "If only *she* would give me her love!"

"The complaint of so many lesbian women was that so few of them could find real friends in adolescence," write the

American psychologists Gundlach and Riess in their report of a study of over 200 normally adapted women suffering from this complex.[8] The inner "complaining child" keeps feeding herself with the very same feelings she had in her youth: inferiority, loneliness, self-pity, and an insatiable craving.

SEVEN

How the Homosexual Complex Works

E XPLAINING WHAT HOMOSEXUAL LOVE really is understandably meets with often indignant resistance. "Why am I not allowed to become happy the way I am?" is the predictable dramatic cry. The question however is not whether or not it is allowed, but whether or not it is viable. Many people with this orientation are no more prepared to let themselves be deprived of their illusory feelings than alcoholics or drug addicts are to let themselves be deprived of their stimulants.

From clinical experience and review of the literature, we can draw some general statements about the functioning of the homosexual complex in both men and women:

1. *Seeking for a lover is repetitive.* Although homosexually inclined women have on average longer relationships than homosexually inclined men, in neither case do their partnerships last over the years. The neurotic addiction to feelings of unfulfilled longing—in other words, neurotic complaining—has them in its grip and forces them to go after new illusions for ever.

2. *Homosexual longings are transitory and superficial.* Homosexual longings and the associated longings for warmth and compassion can be experienced as the most beautiful and deepest in a person's life. Yet this is self-deception. Homo-

75

sexual feelings, sometimes extolled as "pure love," as more profound than marital love, in fact have hardly anything to do with real love. They are self-centered love. This love is an asking, even a begging for love and attention. This is clear from the way homosexual partnerships usually end. The partner is there to fulfill the infantile ego's needs but is not really loved for his or her own being. As a result, there may be clutching to the other on one side and lack of real interest and indifference on the other. It is remarkable how these people may speak of their past relationships—without emotion, like children who threw away a toy they are not interested in anymore.

3. *The homosexually inclined and other neurotics suffer from compulsive self-pity.* Not all of them express their self-pity and complaining tendency in dramatic words and verbal complaints. If one comes to know them a little better, however, self-pitying overtones are nearly always clearly perceptible. They quickly think in terms of problems and worries; some are evidently overemotional, others more the whining and puling type, some are hypercritical of themselves or others; some regularly complain about physical discomfort (which they dramatize); some suffer from depressions, regularly pass through "nervous crises," or complain about loneliness, apathy, disturbed human contacts, and so on. Genuine cheerfulness and gaiety are the exact opposite of this complaining sickness. If it is true that some homosexuals play the role of the jester, the funnyman, one will on closer inspection recognize the depressed, self-pitying child behind this game-playing. That may be a puerile way of drawing admiring attention to the infantile ego. There is always an underlying restlessness.

4. *The homosexually oriented have a hunger for attention, which they can channel in various ways.* They may cling to others to absorb their attention. They may present themselves unconsciously as victims, appealing for help and protection to others' compassionate feelings. Some may impose themselves

on their environment, others tyrannize their environment as a real child can do sometimes. In the first place, they seek attention from a desired partner, but this quest for attention may have been generalized as an important way of relating to other people.

5. *Ego-centeredness is another universal neurotic characteristic.* That implies that in great part, feeling and thinking center around the ego, resulting in reduced genuine interest in and love for others. "My husband consumes others in his surroundings," a wife of a married homosexual man once said to me. "But he is unable to give love himself; he doesn't know what it is." The more predominant the homosexual complex is in a person's emotional life, the more fitting this description.

6. *The "complaining child" in the adult keeps the emotional life at an immature level in other areas than the sexual.* The emotional infantilism of people with a homosexual complex make them behave and think like children and in fact to repress normal emotional growth to a degree that depends on the strength of the complex.

7. *Having partially remained a child includes the relationship to the parents.* Therefore men with this complex have more often than not some "mother bond" or retain a reproachful, hostile attitude toward their father because of a "negative father bond." Similar rules apply to the lesbian woman. The fixated bond with the parents may contain ambivalent elements: someone can dependently cling to his mother and at the same time tend to pick quarrels with her in order to discharge his irritation about her.

8. *The "inner child of the past" preserves infantile attitudes and feelings in regard to the opposite sex.* The homosexual man may continue hating women as the adolescent of the past looked upon them as intruders in his life, or as rivals who would steal his comrades, or simply as "those silly girls" who are the spoilers in the boys' world. He may still feel inferior and fearful in front of them, feeling ashamed of his insufficient manliness. He may also continue viewing certain women as the protect-

ing, mothering, attention-giving figures, not as adult female human beings to whom he should relate as an adult man. On similar grounds, the "girl in the lesbian woman" may continue viewing men through the colored glasses of hatred, envy, fear, or annoyance.

9. *The homosexually oriented have difficulties in fully accepting their so-called gender identity.* The man experiences manly things as not belonging to him; the lesbian woman feels uneasy in things feminine. It is, however, incorrect to think that these men, deep inside, feel like women, or that lesbian women are inwardly men.

10. *Finally, it is not superfluous to note that a homosexual complex dwells within a total personality.* The person as a whole is more than his infantile personality, although some homosexually oriented people may indeed impress one as very immature. If we look more attentively, we will discover that every homosexually afflicted man or woman has many adult qualities and tendencies. Because our study concerns the infantile part of their personality, we may give the mistaken impression that we are dealing with completely sick persons. In fact, the therapist deals with, and in great part relates to, precisely the adult part of the homosexual personality, and it is from this part that we can expect realistic self-insight, good will, and other curative powers. The adult personality is also the more interesting of the two. It is living; the infantile ego on the other hand is more like a mechanism, rigid and stereotyped. In everyday life, we mostly see some mixture of the mature and the childish personalities.

Bisexuality flows from this double personality structure. The sexual orientation from the adult part, as far as it has been developed, is directed to the mature object of sexuality, the opposite sex. The "pitiable child" on the other hand pulls sexuality to his immature objects. Since one part of the bisexual's personality suppresses the other, it is evident that the heterosexuality of these persons is not full-fledged.

EIGHT

The Road to Change

S HOULD A PERSON with a homosexual orientation compel himself to have heterosexual interests or heterosexual behavior? It would be wrong to approach the matter in that way. As I see it, some self-forcing is perhaps desirable in one respect: to make an honest effort to search oneself, without repressing unwelcome insights or distorting certain realities of which one can be aware if one wills. And subsequently, having acquired certain insights into neurotic habits and especially motivations (ego-centeredness, for instance), the homosexually inclined person must face the decision to combat them, at any rate, to restrain them.

The process of change by the help of some form of psychotherapy can lead to quite satisfactory results; however, the outcome is dependent upon many things. The influential factors include: the client's motivation to change, his persistence, sincerity to himself, the overall strength of his neurosis, and social influences such as encouragement by others (as opposed to living alone, not being part of a social group). Real and profound change is in principle possible. According to reports I have read and to the stories of some former homosexuals I have heard and examined myself, a radical change is also sometimes obtained with the help of a religious "method." In every case of real change I know of, however, this came about after relatively long work and only in extremely exceptional cases abruptly in the form of a psychological miracle. Moreover, I believe the growth process in all these cases followed roughly the same pattern, whether they were produced by psychotherapy or other approaches. Some cases of cures without formal psychotherapy will be presented in the following chapter.

The change process is comparable to climbing the stairs when the end is not clearly visible. You do not exactly know where you will end up; but every stair climbed means improvement, progress. Beforehand, we should not worry too much about how far we eventually might come. Certainly, it is not realistic to see marriage as the ultimate goal for everyone with this complex who enters therapy. Theoretically, to be emotionally ripe for marriage (including the sexual emotions) is the most perfect goal. That can often be attained, but perhaps as often not—at least not for a longer period of time. We should bear in mind that homosexually inclined people often want to be married on the basis of infantile complaints, such as the complaint of not being like the others. Thus, marriage is desired not for itself but as an infantile way to catch up with "them." Infantile complaining about being lonely may be another chief motive for the wish to be married. To begin with, the neurotic attachment to the complaint "I am not married" must be undone. The person must completely accept his situation, his inner situation as well as his social situation.

The first stage of the road to change consists of growing out of the homosexual orientation. That usually takes some years. It will have become clear from the earlier explanations of homosexuality that the homosexual urge itself is only a part of a more complex structure of infantile behavior tendencies. Hence the waning of the homosexual interest parallels the gradual decrease of inferiority feelings and ego-centered self-pity.

A therapist treating someone for homosexual neurosis should begin by learning about the client's past, his childhood and adolescent views of himself, his parents, siblings, and playmates, as well as his homosexual history. These interviews provide the therapist with a global idea of the client's neurosis and nearly always give a good many clues as to his childhood feelings of hurt and inferiority. Thereafter, the therapist should explain the theory of the "complaining child"—one or two "lessons," in fact. Of course, the therapist must tune his language and examples to the educational level of the client. This is quite possible because the crucial ideas lend themselves excellently to being communicated in simple, straightforward, and understandable language.

The therapist must make clear that the process is one of self-insight and struggle for the client, that he has to do the essential hard work himself, and that the role of the therapist is one of providing guidance, like the coach in sports training or like any teacher. We advise the client used to practicing homosexual behavior to suppress his desires for contact, or to break off his relationship with a homosexual partner. Some may be inclined to seek a compromise in that matter; they want to change but, at the same time, to continue their emotionally rewarding contacts. We have to make it clear that in doing so they just satisfy their "inner child's" wishes, feeding their neurosis and thus opposing their expectation of change. Sometimes, such hard advice may be postponed for tactical reasons, but often it is preferable to show that trying to be radical is the shortest way to a change. On the other hand, the therapist must take pains to *dedramatize* many client's complaints: "I am a homosexual, a misfit—I *have* to change! I cannot live any longer in this way; I *have* to be married like the others," and so on. We can explain that the "inner child" takes over the awareness of being different in sexual respect, making a big drama out of it in order to afford himself a large quantity of self-pity.

Self-insight and Struggle

It seems to me very difficult to overcome a homosexual complex without acquiring proper insight into one's motives and a more objective view of one's behavior. Thus the person concerned must get insight into his infantile ego, his self-pity and inner complaining tendencies, his asking for sympathy and appreciation. Increasing self-insight along these lines often engenders a greater inner freedom from being obsessed by the autonomous complex, although it does not suffice in itself to overcome it entirely.

Self-observation and self-analysis for the detection of infantile complaints is progressive. Every individual client discovers his own clues that tell him: "At this moment, or in this feeling or thought, the complaint-drive is at work."

Signs that may warn him of the activity of his "complaining ego" are feelings of unrest, irritation, inferiority, apathy, negative emotions and thoughts, and depressions in general. These impulses are experienced as more or less compulsive, as coming from outside one's own ego ("It seized me," "I was assailed by . . . ," etc.). Every client learns to recognize his "self-pitying child" by its individual peculiarities. The main theme of complaining is specific in every individual case, and there are always individual expressions of the main theme of complaining. These chief complaints are repeated in the adult mind.

Many people being treated for a homosexual neurosis will come to realize that a chronic complaint drive is going on in their emotions. It is clearly observable, or they can see it as an accompanying negative emotional overtone, often spoiling positive feelings and experiences. These individuals increasingly become aware that their unhappy feelings are not caused by the problems of their life, external situations, or other persons, but by the negative force within themselves.

Of course the client must be honest with himself if he is to profit from our method of self-observation and self-analysis. It is not flattering for one's infantile ego to have to admit time and again that one was feeling, thinking, or acting like a child, and even more, that one indulged in self-pity. Fully admitting this means that no excuses or explanations, no "yes, but's" are sought, and that one refrains from blaming persons or "the circumstances." To overcome resistance to full recognition of "poor-me" feelings, the client must deal an occasional blow to his childish ego-importance. This way, step by step, the childish, ego-centered complaining attitude becomes clearer and less of a theoretical construction.

When the person has gained self-insight, a period of work or struggle commences. The adult part of the person, his will, tries to stop the recognized infantile tendencies in one way or another, with the methods that seem appropriate. The strength of the complex diminishes as ego-centered habits of thinking and acting are no longer "fed," in particular, as infantile self-pity is counteracted.

Inevitably, the well-intended person with a homophile orientation will find the obstacle of pleasure addiction on his way. The homosexual drive has been strongly reinforced in many of them by their satisfying it either with a partner or in their imagination (masturbation). To break the habit of giving in to it requires not only insight into its puerile character—however necessary that is—but also willpower and patience. To give in to this infantile habit of self-comforting may be especially alluring on such occasions as moments of stress, humiliation, feeling inferior, or loneliness

As we have seen, the homosexual fantasy was created as an illusory solution of an inner drama and the pleasure of its satisfaction often implies a great deal more than simply sexual gratification. Understandably enough, the resistance to abandoning these puerile sexual gratifications (in fantasy or in homosexual practice) is usually considerable.

If one wants to change in depth, that is, to grow beyond one's infantilism and "puerilism," a continuous effort of the will is called for. At certain times, this means simply saying "no" to tendencies recognized as puerile. At other times, it means that certain things must be done that cost a lot of effort and some courage. As a psychotherapist who is especially intent on detecting expressions of childish self-pity, I often train my clients in applying methods or techniques of humor aimed at the neutralization of the manifold manifestations of this basic neurotic emotion. Smiling and laughing at one's infantile "poor me" and one's infantile complaints can be very effective in undermining its strength. The effectiveness of such techniques—like "hyperdramatization" of the inner child's pitifulness—is dependent on the client's will to use them in his everyday life, however.

The inner struggle that must be waged on the neurotic part of the mind implies several things at the same time. For instance, attention-seeking must be curtailed, the fearful habit to flee from scores of situations and behaviors unlearned, excessive self-indulgence and self-pampering frustrated, distorted views of the self and of others corrected (from infantile to more mature), the addiction to inner complaining cured. Complaints of less intensity may be handled by the techniques of merely stopping them after having consciously recognized them as infantile complaints. This technique is adequate for a great many instances when the person is aware of a negative, whining, or sentimental inner attitude. Others require more sophisticated techniques. Interests in others must be learned or strengthened; the capability to love and to give must be developed. Self-directed humor facilitates all of this. One who learns to treat his childish ego with sound irony diminishes its serious feeling of ego-importance. The less important or pitiable this ego feels, the more the adult personality can prevail, and the more childish discontent will give away to more hopeful and happier feelings. The person grows less weak in his own eyes, more stable, more optimistic, more quiet.

Hyperdramatization

We have had success in applying several techniques of self-humor in order to overcome infantile tendencies, especially the manifestations of infantile self-pity. The goal of self-humor is to replace a complaint by its opposite—a smile or a laugh. In general, the goal is to neutralize the "inner child's" importance. Self-humor has great curative powers. It helps the person recognize—emotionally and not merely intellectually—certain distortions and inadequacies in his thinking and behavior. It is, therefore, an excellent antidote against a variety of neurotic impulses. Self-humor, like humor in general, is disarming. Mere rational understanding and even a clear observation of one's infantile strivings and emotions—the goals of self-observation and self-analysis—fail to rid the sufferer of neurotic patterns. We need the support of emotional forces that can counteract the strong infantile emotions of complaining—attention-seeking, the wish to be important, and so on. The emotion released by smiling and laughing has the capacity to reach the infantile ego.

The client who is able to recognize the working of his "child" in everyday life can profit from self-humor techniques. He is trained to apply them on the spot, after having recognized an expression of infantile complaining. He then imagines his "little child" as standing before him in the flesh, or visualizes himself in his imagination as the "child" he was in his past. He starts talking to this "child," like someone who exaggeratedly pities another. He tells the "child" how enormously pitiful he is; accumulating a series of fantasized reasons for his complaining, he paints before this "child's" eyes a super-drama (hyper-drama) surrounding the complaint. Let me give a small example to give the flavor of this technique.

A homosexual client felt slighted by his boss who had preferred another person to represent him at a business meeting. The verbalized feeling of self-pity was: "My boss finds *me* worthless and does not like *me*." This complaint had a side-branch: a feeling of jealousy for his colleague. After realizing that this was his "little boy," the man hyperdramatized as follows: "Poor kid, you are damned right in crying so many tears about this maltreatment. This really was a case of ruthless violence against an innocent child. You, who are always working so hard without any praise whatsoever, were summoned by your boss with a roar, as if he were calling his dog. Trembling all over, you stood there before him in front of your colleagues who were all of them seated in comfortable armchairs. One, the Preferred Colleague, was seated in a specially decorated chair, a big, expensive cigar (a present from the boss) in his mouth, smiling condescendingly while you approached. Then the boss solemnly fetched a scroll, broke its seals, and started reading aloud: 'Hereby I, Mr. X., declare this miserable misfit (you!) completely unfit to represent me. I express my feelings of deepest disgust towards him. Fortunately, however, there is around here a Man of smashing superiority who compensates for this heap of rags. Colleague Y.! . . .' Then, everybody cheers at colleague Y., throws flowers at him, and opens bottles of champagne for him, while laughing at you, and throwing rotten eggs at you. You stood there, your shirt soaked by tears. You finally fell on your knees and crawled out of the room into the cold outside, where your cries and tears mingled with the streaming rain..." The man might continue, if necessary, with a dramatic visualization of the triumph of his colleague. For instance, he could picture this man riding past him in a Rolls Royce with a chauffeur. The complainer, in his worn-out and shabby clothes, had to suffer the humiliation of having the colleague open the car window and drop ash from his cigar on his head.

The client could see how it was understandable that his feeling of being slighted was followed by a homosexual longing—a reaction of self-comfort. A possible hyperdramatization for this secondary, complaint-propelled wish would have been: "Yes, you really need one thing now, and that is genuine, warm love, showers of it, in fact. A warm arm around your shoulder, two manly but still deeply moved eyes looking at you in deep commiseration; a friend who whispers in your ear that you may forever sit on his knees, your scrawny arm around his neck, while his broad, hairy, muscled hand caresses your sickly baby face, etc." The client learns to build his own repertory of hyperdramatization stories and scenes and to use them whenever he notices an infantile complaint. In fantasy, everything is allowed; he may invent the most absurd situations according to his personal sense of the comic, provided they bear directly on the felt complaint. He also learns to apply variants and short-forms of this technique. He treats his "child," for instance, as "my poor boy." For example, "That critical remark they made about you was awful! Now the President will announce a Day of National Mourning on your behalf!" or more simply: "Poor boy! This will be your death!" The more vividly he sees the imagined scene before his eyes, the more exaggeratedly pitiful he sees his "child" at the moment of the complaining, the better it penetrates. Successful hyperdramatizations make a complaint evaporate quickly or gradually. Every approach that elicits smiling or laughing about a complaint is advisable. The method is even applicable with manifestations of infantile, overcompensatory pride. For example: "You are wonderful indeed. Your performance (remark, presentation, etc.) was breath-taking. I can aready see the statue that will be erected here right on this spot. You, on a big horse, like Napoleon, your hand slipping with nonchalance into your waistcoat . . ." Easy as it may seem, regularly practicing self-humor requires a strong determination. Smiling about one's pitiable ego is about the last thing one likes doing at the moment one is beset by infantile complaining.

Recovery

The growth out of the complex takes the following pattern. At first, the obsessive character of the infantile emotions and behavior tendencies decreases. Depressions, anxieties, fears, worries, inferiority feelings, and homosexual longings become more manageable. Self-confidence, including gender self-confidence, is on the upswing—which means no more, after all, than that the inner child's "poor me" becomes less important, that the person does not take this ego so seriously anymore. Homosexual interests fluctuate for a long time, but are felt as less and less overwhelming. They fade away undramatically, as a function of the overall increase of a more positive and mature emotionality.

The sexual change should be regarded as part of the total emotional reorientation. Homosexuals who want to be "cured" often have an understandably narrow view of what has to be changed and tend to pay almost exclusive attention to the changes in their sexual feelings. It is true that a real and deep sexual change reflects changes in other mental areas as well, but the effects of a therapy or self-therapy (which our procedure is for a large part) should not primarily be measured in strictly erotic terms. Changes in sexual feelings are more or less "by-products" and will certainly appear when—and to the degree that—the client's "complaining child" has been starved. It is not advisable, therefore, for the therapist or the client to be too sexuality-oriented in their attention and discussions. The principal yardsticks of change are the level of the client's complaining and of his general emotional infantilism. Of course, changes in these factors exert an influence on the erotic domain, but the relationship is hierarchical: the deeper the client changes in the fundamental dimensions of infantilism and self-pity, the more radical his sexual reorientation will be.

Then, perhaps in the majority of the cases, the person goes through an intermediate stage in which the homosexual orientation is already almost nonexistent, but heterosexuality is hardly awakened. This in-between period may last for years in some cases. The person "discovers" the opposite sex either gradually or suddenly, after the maturation process of these intermediate years. Some fall in love one or two times and wind up marrying; for others it takes a long time before they are able to maintain a steady heterosexual love relationship. The whole process thus is a kind of self-reeducation. Ups and downs, and occasional relapses, usually are part of it. There may be moments—or even longer periods—of loss of hope. The course of the process varies widely in particulars from individual to individual.

The homosexually inclined, even if they are in principle willing to change, initially have serious doubts whether there are realistic chances of a profound improvement. These are periodically returning doubts, notwithstanding clearly observable progress, and they only die away when the change in feelings has become much more obvious. Doubts flare up every time these people hear or read the standard stories on homosexuality: once a homosexual, always a homosexual. Looking more closely, we shall see that these doubts are just another variant of neurotic complaining: "I shall never be normal; it is my fate; poor me!" Therefore, hope and faith are excellent barriers to these harmful thoughts that are a drain on the person's enthusiasm and energy. A realistic stand is also a good remedy for these paralyzing doubts: "In any case, I see that I have to fight what I have recognized as childish, as wrong, and if I persist in doing so I trust that there will be progress, even if that amounts to no more than moderate change."

We can establish over and again that the one who makes the effort becomes happier. Let him not be obsessed with the question of whether or not he will reach 100 percent, but let him be content with every step forward and enjoy it. That is, after all, the mentality that appears to bring the client closest to his goal.

Working at oneself, let alone fighting one's undesirable, self-centered habits and attachments, is not a popular issue in our permissive and overindulgent age. Certainly there has been a great deal written on psychological "therapy," and a great variety of theories and therapeutic techniques have been developed. Only a small part of all this, however, aims at actually struggling with one's faults and frailties in order to overcome them. Psychotherapy is seldom little more than teaching the client to abandon himself to his puerile egoism, even to immorality. The specious exhortation "accept yourself" becomes then tantamount to surrender to immaturity on the one hand and repression of one's "better me" on the other. (This "better me" or adult ego may have a healthy longing for a more mature existence, it may have normal feelings of annoyance in the face of the infantile ego, even normal guilt feelings.) Like it or not, the human psychological reality *is* that we must make a choice between opposing tendencies. A plea for "acceptance of yourself" is often a plea for childishness. The alternative, to work at yourself, is more difficult, but it is the only way to inner happiness and peace of mind.

The relatively few people who try to work themselves out of their homosexual orientation do not meet with much public understanding and approval. On the contrary, they find discouragement wherever possible. I hope that this little work can help them refute the false slogan "you can do nothing about it."

NINE

Change without Psychotherapy

B EFORE DESCRIBING THE RESULTS of the "anticomplaining" therapy just outlined, I would like to offer some cases of persons cured of homosexuality by other means. In this chapter I will describe two cases that have appeared in published accounts. They show how the same psychological dynamics used in anticomplaining therapy are at work in other situations.

The first case is that of an exlesbian woman who told her story to a Dutch psychiatrist, himself a homosexual who propagates "acceptance" as the solution, who reacted in one of his articles to that effect.[1] Fortunately, the psychiatrist honestly published his interview with her, remarking that "she made a perfectly normal impression. Normal emotionality, a relaxed laugh and adequate seriousness. Perfectly reliable." The case should impress the more as it is offered as a real cure by a man who himself is more than skeptical about the remediability of homosexuality. "Although your article does not offer much hope, I still was cured at my thirty-seventh year. Can you imagine my happiness? It is not comparable with anything whatsoever. Thirty-seven years of sorrow, misery, help-seeking, praying, hoping, etc., not seeing anything in the world except your own deeply hurting misery. With the rock-firm conviction that, after so many years, you have to drag it with you until your death," she said. Besides her appeal to hope and faith, this fragment contains a very instructive little phrase which we should not pass by lightly: "not seeing anything in the world except your own deeply hurting misery." It is a beautiful epitaph for her former neurotic life, summarizing its essential element, the excessive self-centeredness of obsessive "poor me" feelings. She views her former attitude with proper irony, seeming to smile at her dramatic poor-me of the past.

How did it all come about? She was a nurse, frequently falling in love with older women ("it preoccupied me completely, it was like a cloud around me"), eventually attempting suicide after one of those affairs led to a failure (she never practiced homosexual contacts). The woman felt completely lost, desperately wanting to get rid of her obsessions. Perhaps such a painful depression prepares one for a change: it cannot be worse. In this state of mind, she met an understanding but at the same time realistic priest, who although listening sympathetically to her complaints, made some pungent observations that had shocked her. "Every time I left him, I felt as I were turned upside down, brainwashed. But once he said something I shall never forget: 'Child, you are not mature at all, you're only about sixteen years of age.' That same night in my room, at 9:30, I saw it all, at once." She clearly locates her "change" at that hour of healing self-insight. A child she was, behaving and feeling like a child. The man had opened her eyes to her "inner child," and from the moment of its recognition, her cure was on the way.

Having seen her childish personality, she now set out vigorously to overcome its many facets. This she called her "adaptation," the "switch" to "society as it was, whereas before I lived in a society like I saw it." She had to discover reality, while she had lived in too subjective, emotional a world before. "Before, you *are* lived." This clearly expresses her neurotic obsession by reality-blurring emotionality. The neurotic lives in the atmosphere of complaint-ruled emotions, thus, in a distorted reality. "People must have thought of me: What a naive person she is!"—really *a child*, judging her environment from her childish viewpoints and feelings. The "adaptation" which followed upon her recognition of being a child "perhaps lasted about a year," which is very rapid in my eyes.

Not only does this woman describe her change as an abandonment of her childishness, but also as the disappearance of an inferiority complex. "I had a serious inferiority complex," she says. "Before, everything and everybody was always superior to me." In addition, she relates the change in her feelings of being ashamed. Before, she felt ashamed about things that she did not need to be ashamed of: these feelings were inferiority feelings. Inferiority feelings also manifested themselves as exaggerated submissiveness. "Formerly, I always did everything for everyone. I still do things for people, but there is always a 'but.' Perhaps it is idiotic too, that I never thought about myself before." Her inferiority feelings took the form, "I am not good at all. I have to serve everybody because I am the least of them."

She mentions her former jealousy, her former lack of real *feelings* of sympathy for suffering people, despite her helpful behavior (egocentricity), her changed attitude towards God (formerly, a punishing figure inspiring fear in her, and now filling her with gratitude and respect), her former nervous twists of the mouth, her walking anxiously near the walls of the houses instead of in the middle of the pavement. "Nothing has stayed the same." Here we find the common experience that a cured homosexual takes on a "brand-new personality"; the cure of homosexuality is primarily an overall emotional change or a personality change.

How about the erotic change of this exlesbian? "Formerly, men did not stir anything in me, nothing at all. And I did not even think about marriage. When I grew older, the sexual relationship between man and woman was strange to me; I could not understand it nor feel anything of it. A man provoked in me about as much as a cat"—from which quotation one may safely conclude that she had also remained a child, not even an adolescent, in her erotic development. The first shock of recognition of her fixation to childishness unlocked great joy and relief. "The whole world was mine, I felt so very happy. I did not have a desire for women, nor for men." The course of events is classic for many cases-to-be-cured: cheerfulness sweeps away homoerotic interests (which are complaints, therefore the opposite of joy and happiness), the client passes through a stage in which eroticism in either direction seems absent: "only in the years afterwards the erotic interest in men has gradually appeared." Not before the neurotic complaint-based sexuality has disappeared can adult heterosexual emotions freely unfold, and, as this woman says, this may be a process which takes some time; it appears to be a process of growth. When heterosexuality awoke, it had the characteristics of an adolescent's being interested in many men at about the same time, many infatuations: "I sort of wanted to marry all men at the same time." At last, this stage was left, she calmed down and married her present husband. In comparison with her former obsessive sexual preoccupations she feels she "has outgrown a little bit all the sexual stuff," which, certainly if we take into account that the woman is forty-four years old at the time of the investigation, is to be interpreted as a sign of maturity. Of her former lesbian interest she says: "It is like a leg which has been cut off and that simply cannot grow back. I cannot yet grasp how I could have been that way for all those years; I cannot even understand it any more." This real change—her former lesbian feelings have become hardly imaginable to her—had already lasted seven years when she made this statement, a very acceptable period of follow-up.

Summing up the important cure-promoting elements which may be isolated from her history, anticomplaining therapists will recognize a number of familiar factors: a whole-hearted refusal to identify herself irremediably as a homosexual, leading to an optimal open-mindedness to any cues that might further a change; recognition of her "child," or self-insight;

the struggle to overcome infantile sets in thought and habits; honesty to herself; and confidence in her "therapist" who happened to be the right man for her, observing her infantilism and giving her the right kind of understanding and support.

Religious Conversion

Some people claim a profound change from their homosexual orientation by religious conversion. In general, we had better remain skeptical of these stories because of the sources of possible self-deception within the neurotic's personality which may make him believe in what he ardently wishes to believe; until, of course, a critical investigation has overruled our doubts. I have examined several persons who claimed to have been "cured" by religious conversion but in reality were not. In fact, they so vehemently rejected and disapproved of their homosexual interests, or they unconsciously played the role of the "changed homosexual," clinging so much to their newfound religion, that it seemed that their neurosis had simply shifted from one type of obsession to another. Typically these persons would not answer matter-of-fact questions about their current erotic life or about the exact nature of their sexual feelings and would instead start a sermon, as if to persuade others—and themselves—that they had really changed. This kind of self-deception, as a matter of fact, is not the dubious privilege of those who tried the religious way in order to change. One should be attentive to it in the course of every psychotherapeutic process as well; the client sometimes wishes too compulsively to be normal, and on the basis of this, he tries to persuade himself that he already has changed. The religious homosexual may, moreover, egotistically enjoy belonging to a religious group or even being an important member of it (as the "convert," the "preacher").

Nevertheless, I know several persons whose cure, brought about by an active religious life, I could verify after repeated conversations in which I carefully analyzed their feelings and attitudes. They talked quietly and without inhibitions about their emotions and attitudes; they did not evade direct answers to direct questions and did not manifest any exaggerated urge to persuade me. I think these cases are perhaps more numerous than we would presume, because many of them prefer to stay anonymous and not be public examples of "the converted-and-cured-homosexual." In some of these cases I was quite sure that every, however little, homosexual impulse had disappeared many years past and that their feelings were hetero-sexualized. In addition, they had been liberated from much emotional turmoil, many depressions and worries, and had become considerably less self-centered in their thoughts and feelings. Characteristically, they could tell about their past with a sense of humor. All of them stressed the importance of the will—"As a homosexual, you can complain, wish to change, etc.," one of them said, "but in reality it is too beautiful for you to really want to get rid of it. Your will is half-baked, that is the big problem." Being questioned a few years, or in two of these cases, even many years after the change in homosexual orientation, all these persons said that the overall emotional change in them had been gradual and they still could experience some inferiority feelings in some situations at present, although without being seriously disturbed by them, experiencing them as only minor intrusions in their sense of well-being.

From my conversations with "religiously" changed homosexuals I generalize that it had been highly important to them to find faith, certainty in life, a deep sense in their personal life and that this discovery made them feel happy, provided them with a great relief and a source of joyful emotions. This made them see their homosexual problem as a minor thing, stripping it of the paramount importance it formerly had in their consciousness: they stopped worrying and complaining about it. Then, they realized that it was important to seek and carry out the will of God and not their own: process of "deegocentrization" was set in motion. "I did not serve God by my complaining," an exlesbian woman told me. "I tried to do what I thought he wanted me to do, and that was a whole program. This indeed was the thing that gradually but radically changed my life." We can understand the salutary effect of this attitude-change. The neurotic, being an "I-person," primarily thinking about himself, submits his will to the will of God, that is, towards goals outside himself, and thus is liberated from himself. In the process, he undoubtedly will discover how much his orientation had been towards his own self (his *infantile* self, we would say). The reorientation from this "self" will often be difficult and painful, because it presupposes the sacrifice of a number of things that were very dear to this infantile "I." Moreover, it presupposes meditation, prayer, and the study of the Bible in order to learn the "will of God" which is to be the new goal in life.[2]

The homosexual obsessions or longings disappear from the person's consciousness in the course of this process, and heterosexual interests arise, without the person being so much concentrated on this subject. The real change is felt as something very nuclear in the personality and the changes in sexual interests as the more or less natural consequences of this basic change. As a result, one cannot speak in such genuine cases of "sublimation" of homosexuality, which essentially is no more than distraction of the attention, an explanation which seems to be more adequate for the cases of "religious neurosis" we discussed above.

John V.

As an example of the healing influence of religious conversion on homosexuality I will quote from the booklet *I Am No Longer "That Way,"* which contains the history of the change from homosexuality to heterosexuality of a young Dutchman, John V.[3] More than ten years after his fundamental change had been reasonably consolidated and after he had been married for many years, I could convince myself of the genuineness of his change. He told me that he had been occasionally troubled by minor neurotic impulses for a long time after his basic change.

John V. is very open and honest about his feelings. He admitted that he could in principle imagine possibly relapsing into a homosexual contact in exceptional circumstances, but that he still thought it to be very improbable that such a thing would occur. "I want to say," he elucidated, "that I cannot answer your question: 'Can you not even *imagine* anymore that you would have a homosexual feeling, even in extraordinary circumstances?' with a straight 'No' and neither does the imagination of a homosexual contact inspire me with physical disgust." According to the most stringent criteria, then, his change cannot be regarded as perfect, but in view of the nearly complete absence of any homosexual impulse in his fantasy or consciousness during many years as well as the presence of normal heterosexual interests, the total results cannot but impress the unprejudiced student of homosexuality. I shall quote from John V.'s autobiographical booklet, not because his change is the most radical one I have ever seen, but because his narrative contains observations on some phenomena which occur frequently in the course of a homosexual's change, like his wild, desperate, and infantile surrender to what he saw as his salvation (the pentecostal movement[4]), his periods of deep despair as well as sky-high joy, and, after all, the fact that the change took time and consisted of a normal growth or learning process which can easily be translated into psychological terms.

Having been diagnosed a "primary" or "nuclear" and irremediable homosexual by a well-known sexologist and living as a committed homosexual, this man in his late twenties could not feel emotionally satisfied by his homosexual friendships, inwardly experiencing them as something contrary to his religious feelings. Religious feelings aside, however, he discovered that the homosexual way of life was unable to make him happy.

> I had learned to experience it in a stormy way. But it had failed to bring me profound happiness.... "Still, love is not sinful," I claimed. But inwardly I became empty. I hardly read the Bible if at all and was extraordinarily neurotic ... I was over-tired ... hardly ventured into company.

An interview with a Christian who said that he himself had been a homosexual for many years but had been freed from his obsessions made him realize that his way of life, his relationship with his friend, was sinful. "It seemed as if at that moment there was a great light in the room, causing the darkness to disappear from my life," but already the same night he thought it impossible to ever change and fall in love with a girl; he even found the thought of it aversive. Yes and no—the inner struggle of so many homosexuals who are chained to their seemingly "natural" impulses. Even so, he somehow was aware that he should break off his "sinful" relationship with his friend. Many homosexuals will recognize themselves in what he remembers:

> The last nights before finally leaving my friend, which I spent with him in Bergen op Zoom [a Dutch city] were horrible. At the last moment I thought not to be able to cope with the rupture between us. For three years we had lived together and loved each other. I was hypernervous and cried a lot. But it was as if a supernatural power enabled me to disengage myself from him. Upon my arrival in Rotterdam, I felt relaxed for the first time in many years, as if a heavy burden had been taken from my shoulders.

He then went through a period of alternating hope and despair, praying to God when he felt his homosexual urge and longed for his former friend, and seeking support from preachers in the pentecostal movement. In spite of a certain criticism he felt towards these people, he submitted himself to having hands laid on him, believing he would receive the Holy Spirit. At the same time, a Christian married couple supported and encouraged him, reinforcing his faith that he really would, by the help of God, overcome his homosexuality. These things gave him the strength to destroy radically all remembrances of his homophile past (objects, books, photographs) and to persist in his complete rejection of every homosexual thought or impulse.

> About two months after my liberation I also started looking at girls with different eyes. I discovered that they are anything but inferior. More and more I became conscious of my manhood. God made me discover the beauty of women. I began being attracted to them. You are slowly developing in that direction, I thought. Similarly, I began viewing the normal man-woman relationship more and more in the right way.

Here, John V. repeats what can be observed in many homosexuals on their way to normalcy: at first, the homosexual interest diminishes, accompanied by a general emotional change towards positive emotions. Then, after the lapse of some time, the first heterosexual feelings set in. Note that the man tells this in connection with his strengthened feeling of being a man, that is, in correlation with the weakening of his complaint of being inferior as a man. His view of girls is transposed to a more mature one, than that seen through the little boy's eyes: naughty creatures from a different world, not from the world of "the boys with each other."

John V. had his periodical relapses, like most recovering neurotics, sometimes very vehement. But he persisted in his strategy: trying to live as he thought God required him to, praying in moments of "temptation" and using his will power. Some years afterwards, he married the girl he fell in love with, and today—ten years afterwards—he is a quiet, reasonable, happy man. The last times his homosexual impulses had appeared, he told me, they were short-lived thoughts arising in the wake of some childish frustration, as when his fiancee was visited by a girlfriend and he felt a lack of her attention.

As to the impression he makes at the present time: he does not complain, nor is he inclined to pathetic sentiments, while his booklet makes it very clear that once he was a highly dramatic, complaint-ridden personality. As I remarked above, I would not explain the process of deneurotization of John V. as something supernatural. Religious emotions, as every psychologist who is familiar with the works of William James or Maslow knows, belong to the most drastic experiences that can affect a person's whole emotional life. In the case of John V., these experiences are described as moments of a breakthrough of *hope* and elated *joy*; in themselves, they did not neutralize his homosexual neurosis, but they gave him a positive emotional basis from which to start, optimism: feelings of happiness, and an enlightened vision of his life as meaningful. Moreover, he was given the faith that his homosexuality would be reversible, not being in agreement with his real nature as a man created by God. Finally, his religious conviction fueled his rejection of all homophile feelings and all things connected with them—they were felt as sinful, negative, and miserable. We should not underestimate the last factor, because the homosexual neurotic is very much attached to his longings as to something precious, great, beautiful, conducive to happiness. As a result, we must establish that a religious conversion can afford a homosexual the hope and energy he wants for his struggle.

The homosexual who wants to be cured is in bad need of those ingredients, as his underlying despair is considerable, his addiction powerful, his will to fight often half-hearted and undermined by the negativism inherent to his self-pity compulsion. Religious experiences can temporarily place him in a new inner world, but thereafter, he will have to fight persistently, because they do not definitely sweep his neurosis away. They serve as powerful sources of energy and motivation, while the psychological process of change itself is one of constant and radical "starvation" of the neurotic emotions, a deconditioning process, one might say. Therefore, it is not astounding that it will take some time, while relapses (large and small) are part of it. As John V. himself observes with respect to his awakening heterosexuality: "You develop slowly into that." The religious experience seems to trigger "inner resources": willpower, insight, and positive emotions; they make the person really fight and afford him the necessary motivational strength to continue. It would be unscientific to neglect these empirical facts, though I can imagine that some scientific psychologists might resist looking at them seriously.

A cure like John V.'s is not a religious miracle, taking place in a flash. There are homosexual people who confuse their religious experiences with a psychological cure or who preach instant cures by religious conversion ("faith healing"). In my opinion, they are bound to be disillusioned. They pray and pray and pray, but "nothing happens to them" as they erroneously expect. Or in other cases, they spasmodically make themselves believe that they have "chased away their devil." The simple proof of a cure, however, is a sober analysis of a person's whole emotional life, including its sexual part. A really cured homosexual is everything but a cramped, hysterical, or fanatical personality. He feels relaxed, is realistic in his self-observations and has nothing to hide from himself.

Cases of homosexuals changed without psychotherapy remind us that "more roads than just one lead to Rome." Still, these exhomosexuals seem to have roughly followed the same psychological track; they somehow "starved" their infantile self-pity drive with its concomitants as infantile ego-centeredness, inferiority feelings, and worries. All these case histories confirm, moreover, the statement of Hatterer that the "will to change" is a crucial condition for improvement and that the process of change itself implies a struggle, that it is a will-steered growth-process.[5] The phenomena encountered in the course of this process are virtually universal relapses, periods of despair, growing self-insight, appearance of heterosexual interests only after the homosexual orientation has been overcome in at least the major part, and living through a period of consolidation which can last for several years after the basic change. Nevertheless, we should aim at a more systematic treatment approach that unites the salutary elements analyzed above and makes use of our theoretical understanding of homosexuality as a disease of infantile self-pity. Even the religiously motivated homosexual can profit from these insights in that they provide him with a clear intellectual structure to envisage his neurosis and, beyond that, give him some concrete weapons to fight with, so that he can cover the road he has set about more effectively than without a psychological map and compass. Anticomplaining therapy is such a systematic treatment, and it is time to see how we should read the map it offers and how its compass functions.

TEN

Effects of
Anticomplaining Therapy

THE HOMOSEXUAL NEUROSIS CAN BE OVERCOME, much as any other neurosis can be overcome. The fatalistic idea that this neurosis cannot change is encouraged by spokesmen of the militant homosexual movement and by other advocates of relativistic morality. I do not claim that a radical change in homosexual orientation is easily attainable. No change of a phobic or obsessive-compulsive neurotic is easy. But the possibility of a fundamental change for the better is definitely there. Much depends on the person's sincerity in acquiring self-knowledge and on his will—that splendid, underestimated faculty of the mind.

From extensive analysis of a series of 101 persons I had in treatment,[1] I have derived the following summarizing statements about the effectiveness of our therapy. Of those who continued treatment—60 percent of the total group—about two-thirds reached at least a satisfactory state of affairs for a long period of time. By this is meant that the homosexual feelings had been reduced to occasional impulses at most while the sexual orientation had turned predominantly heterosexual, or that the homosexual feelings were completely absent, with or without predominance of heterosexual interests. Of this group, however, about one-third could be regarded as having been changed "radically." By this is meant that they did not have any more homosexual interests but had normal heterosexual feelings, and in addition that they showed a fundamental change in overall emotionality from negative to positive—from instability to reasonable, normal stability—with a follow-up period of at least two years.

However, the "satisfactory change" does not stand for a fixed mental state. The person may continue to grow slowly and steadily. He usually passes through new emotional crises, of more or less severity, and may profit from life experiences to emotionally integrate at a higher level. It is not exceptional that they quietly progress, despite ups and downs, throughout the years.

For instance, a man who stopped regular contacts with me at this stage of a "satisfactory change" had fallen in love with a girl whom he eventually married. Some twelve years later I renewed contact with him. In reviewing his emotional life of the past period, he told me that he had had an occasional homosexual "fit" during the first years of his marriage, but that these "fits" moved him emotionally much less than they had in the old days. He had felt this as more or less going on outside himself. These short-lived flarings had faded away and, he added, "I cannot remember having any interest in that direction for many years. When I look with some erotic interest at another person besides my wife, it is always a woman. If my marriage were to go under, I would not seek intimate contacts with men, but with women." He had also lived through some times when he was inclined to withdraw into himself, being secretive and down—mostly after marriage frictions. (His wife was also not totally devoid of some infantile mechanisms.) However, he succeeded in recognizing these reaction habits of his as repetitions of his childhood reactions upon feeling disapproved of, and located them as coming from the remnants of his "pitiful little boy." That made him come to grips with his childish whining. When he objectively judged that his wife's behavior had been unreasonable, he was able to draw the conclusion, "That does not give you the right to feel sorry for yourself." To sum up, he had become a great deal more mature in the course of the years. Yet the skeptic will possibly remark that only a third of those who continued treatment radically changed. I agree that these results are still far from perfect, but then, this does not lead to fatalistic interpretation of these findings. I think there is more reason to consider the glass half filled rather than half empty. The radically changed cases—from complete homosexuality to normal heterosexuality—refute the theory that therapy of homosexuality is pointless. Indeed since relatively few homosexuals seriously try to change and few therapists encourage them to do so, the notion that homosexuality is irreversible is a self-fulfilling prophecy. If nobody tries, nobody will succeed. Finally, why would we take a fatalistic attitude toward the possibilities of improvement of homosexuality when an acceptable percentage improves substantially? The results of incidence of recovery from other neuroses is about the same, as is the incidence of recovery from physical diseases that are not yet curable in all instances. Do we give up if we can only be successful in a part of the cases?

In view of all this, I think we may be optimistic about recovery from homosexuality. About twenty percent of homosexuals in treatment do not seem to change perceptibly. Nevertheless, some improvements can be made by these people, even though they are in general highly neurotic and prone to having a multitude of sexual contacts, deep depressions, and feelings that their lives are senseless. For example, I think of a man with whom I have had periodic contacts for more than fifteen years. I am probably the only person with whom he can speak freely. He was extremely neurotic, obsessed with numerous complaints and with homosexual impulses that he always hated. In spite of my skepticism that some progress would be possible after so long a time, he began reporting that he had overcome his deep and suicidal depressions, and that he had to admit that he was generally more quiet and optimistic. He behaved this way too. We may learn from such cases that we should never lose hope. It is not my conviction that only this self-pity-based therapy can change a homosexual neurosis. I am sure, however, that the insights about the "complaining child" and the use of humor techniques can be very helpful for those who are determined to counter their neurosis. These techniques stimulate the salutary powers of the mind: one's sound insights, interest in self-knowledge, and most of all, the power of the will. Such powers probably also operate in nontherapeutically changed homosexuals.

Most homosexually oriented persons possess the homosexual complex in what I would call a "mild form." Also in them, infantile emotionality may have struck deep roots and created strong neurotic habits, but if they would combat it with some perseverance, they would have a favorable prospect of a radical recovery.

To show what anticomplaining therapy can do, I would like to present a few examples from my own experience. The first example is a case with a moderately positive development. It concerns a young man whose progress was laborious; it seems to me to stand for a whole category of similar cases.

Ben

Ben was not yet twenty years of age when he consulted me. Since adolescence he had had erotic fantasies about men of thirty to thirty-five years, particularly when masturbating. He felt not at all attracted to girls, had no friends (no homosexual contacts either), and stayed at home most of the time. His neurotic emotionality was apparent from his facial expression; he looked annoyed and sulky, his posture and demeanor were lax and limp. He had been pampered and overprotected by his mother, to whom he continued to cling. She was excessively preoccupied with him; when I once met her she constantly referred to him in a sentimental way as to "this child." His father had hardly been involved in his upbringing. He was a somewhat withdrawn man who left his son in his wife's hands (she gave the impression that she would have tried to rule him anyway). Mother seemed to adore him, but wanted him to be like what she had in mind. Ben did not dare to speak up to her; he was an outsider at school and could not cope with the other boys as the result of his upbringing. He had withdrawn into a silent, slightly arrogant posture that was, however, unable to conceal his deep feelings of inferiority.

In this sad period he had come to know a friend of his parents, a young married man with cheerful and lively ways. This man happened to pay some attention to Ben as well, and sometimes asked him to accompany his young family on outings. In his childish imagination Ben began idealizing this friend, fantasizing himself in the role of the poor boy that he was in the center of his attention. He thought away, as it were, the man's wife and little son; he became in his own mind the favorite love object of the admired friend who possessed everything to which Ben himself felt inferior. From time to time, these fantasies came to his mind when he masturbated.

Ben wanted to do something about his homosexual orientation that had by that time grown into an obsession. He did not want to give in; he was deeply ashamed by his inclinations, chiefly because he viewed them as just another proof of his being inferior to other men; and he had regular crying spells that bordered on hysteria. He was a lax young man, used to giving in to his wishes and to avoiding whatever could cause him trouble or effort. His attempts at coping with his "inner child," then, were not very firm. Hardships and normal setbacks had always been causes of self-pity with him, and when he gathered that he was to go through a prolonged period of work, he reacted in his usual way.

However slow the changes in this case, small improvements took place. For example, he became less childishly jealous of his colleagues by fighting the complaint in which this feeling was rooted, namely, "I am inferior to them; they get the attention, the esteem, not I—poor me!" He reduced the frequency of his masturbation, in his case clearly an infantile escape that, in spite of its pleasure element, strengthened the self-pity from which it sprang. Trying to counteract his inferiority feelings as to sports, he joined a sports club and encountered there many situations he could see as a challenge. Slowly, he began changing his old habit of leaving decisions to others (mother figures in the first place). Often, however, he did not really defy his mother because of her irritation, and ended up with what was in fact a new capitulation to her will. His fits of depression disappeared completely; not so, however, the underlying, nourishing structure of chronic self-pity. He continued feeling pitiful in the face of daily frustrations, notably feelings of being neglected, being incapable, failing, or being excluded.

This underlying self-pity in multiple forms dawned on him at last when he had been under treatment for more than two years. He became alive to his feeling inferior and pitiable in almost every company, with respect to almost anyone he met. He discovered that it was he himself who took the attitude "I am inferior and pitiful," and who immediately maneuvered himself in the role of the victim, whereas before he had been convinced that it was the world, the others, who treated him as inferior.

Much could be said about a series of small inner discoveries and minor changes. He made a real step forward, for example, when he decided not to dress any longer in certain clothes he had bought out of childish vanity, in order to draw the admiring attention of others. The fight against infantile self-pity and tendency to complain must be fought in everyday life, on occasion of small frustrations, dislikings, impulses of apathy, exaggerated irritations, tiredness after work, and so on. Ben's case was no different. He concentrated on his habit of fleeing responsibilities and complaining that his undertakings would end in failure. He had to become more active. His homophile fantasy expressed by looking for certain types of young men—at least, in his imagination—gradually lost much of its fascination. Naturally, it presented itself again at times when he felt helpless and hopeless. Occasionally feelings of attraction toward girls emerged, especially in his more optimistic moods. He has had a girlfriend of late, although this relationship seems to be rather immature (on both sides, to be sure). I have the impression that Ben places the girl too much in the mother role and is not really in love with her despite some heterosexual interest in her.

His progress on the whole is evident to his therapist and to people who know him well. After about five years, he is more independent and manly, and more optimistic. Homosexual interests are not extinct, although they have lost their intensity and influence over his imagination. He will need another couple of years before he has sufficiently crossed the threshold to adult manhood.

Mr. L.

He is approaching forty and has an intense homosexual life behind him. He hesitates to continue his homosexual way of life because he has lost his belief in the viability of a lasting relationship. He has noticed that, even when he thought at first that he had found the right friend, he invariably got irritated with his friend after a while and broke off the relationship. Why? he wondered. Women on the other hand do not mean much to him, although he gets along well with them on a superficial level.

In his manner, he is overfriendly, obsequious; he hardly dares to give his own opinion and if he expects disagreement with his ideas, he easily complies. He is unduly impressed by aggressive manly types and by authority figures in general. His supervisor at his office, for instance, makes him feel very tense, and he cannot face him when he is angry; on the other hand, he has an excessive admiration for him. Mr L. has occasional depressions and periods when he feels no energy for work.

His mother had been very self-effacing and occupied only a background position in his emotional life, although I had the impression that her way of rearing the boy had been soft and overly careful. It was the father who was the central figure in the home, who decided everything, whose will determined even minor household affairs. Father had been the crucial person in Mr. L.'s youth. He was aggressive in general, and was very exacting and stern toward his children. He had inhibited his son's emotional development. Mr. L. had always felt that his father was down on him. Father was never encouraging; Mr. L. had in fact had the idea that his father considered him the less interesting of the brothers, a softy. His brothers excelled in various sports, while he felt decidedly inferior in that field. Later on, he tried to compensate for this by plunging into car racing, but the inferiority complex did not abate.

Mr. L. could remember a great many sad experiences during adolescence that shaped his eventual inferiority complex: criticisms and ironic remarks by his father, whom he feared and admired at the same time, failures in sports, periods of loneliness in his room, hurt feelings. With them had emerged his longing for appreciation by a fatherly friend. In fact, he had had a good friend in his early twenties, toward whom he had behaved more or less as a slave. The friend, however, had left for another part of the country and eventually got a girlfriend. Mr. L.'s homoerotic dreams of self-comfort intensified.

The process of change up to the moment I cover it here took about three years. For a good while, Mr. L. was divided against himself. He was alive to the impossibility of renewing his life without making a clean sweep that would deal with more than merely the complaints he initially presented: depressive episodes and his incapacity of having lasting homosexual relationships. He began to see through the pattern of his "inner child" and to revitalize many childish behaviors: in his case feeling quickly insulted and humiliated, feeling inferior as to demeanor and performance to other males in his surroundings, indulging in self-pity when he was alone in his room, being overly irritated at unimportant occasions, and complaining about his physical state when in effect he was healthy and strong. His sincerity was a great help. He would react touchily when certain realities of his life and motives were exposed, but saw some truth in the remarks I made in spite of his resistance. He also applied the techniques of self-directed irony and humor toward the manifestations of his infantile "poor me" at many occasions in his daily life.

He became more independent among other men. We did not spend much time discussing his homosexual feelings and outings, only his nonsexual behavior in front of the partners he still occasionally contacted when in therapy. It was clear to him that his homosexual feelings were a mixture of the daydreaming of a pitiful adolescent, seeking for warmth for his poor inner self and admiration for the other's alleged manliness. He understood that he sought illusory human contacts that had nothing whatsoever to do with love for the yearned-after friend. Precisely in seeking such a friend, he would reinforce his imprisonment in his self-centeredness and therefore make it imposible to feel a durable togetherness. The complaint "I am lonely" had to be repeated. He would predictably throw himself into his isolated position because he could not do without the self-pity inherent in this victim role.

He hesitatingly parted from the homosexual world and from his inner homosexual fantasy world. Occasionally, he relapsed and engaged anew in homosexual contacts, without, however, his former excitement. He became more conscious of the fact that his whole attitude to life and other people had been one of aloofness, of not committing himself to anything, playing the hurt outsider. He therefore became less of a cynic and laid off his superior role-playing. He realized that he should dedicate his life to values after having made up his mind that everything is *not* relative and accepted the belief that his personal life was not devoid of sense, as he had thought before. He recognized that his ability to give himself to others, to love, was small. "Have I ever really loved?" he asked himself. His view of women changed; he started to notice them and to feel stirred by the feminine behavioral and physical qualities of a certain woman. He has the impression that he is growing toward the capacity to have a stable relationship with a woman.

Mr. V.

This young man in his early twenties passed through a roughly similar inner development, including a few pronounced "down" episodes; he fell in love with a young woman after a couple of years of working on himself. The love relationship triggered new difficulties. As soon as he began to desire her, he became aware of the extent of the fear and inferiority feelings he had always had with respect to the opposite sex. His former "adjustment roles" of being the charming and friendly guy collapsed in the personal confrontation with a woman where he was to be the man. At times he panicked anew; he had to struggle for some months with his inferiority feelings and self-pity. There were also moments, however, that he felt relaxed and could identify with his being a man. Then he was also heterosexually aroused, whereas in his distressed moods the heterosexuality seemed flooded.

The first years of his marriage have been good. He has grown steadily away from his infantilisms, his anxieties when confronted with a situation that required independence and some dose of normal aggression, and his giving in too easily to self-pity when something disappointed him. He looks upon his homophile interests, which he had virtually never practiced except in his fantasy, as a puerile tendency that belonged to a past age-stage when he had still to find the right destination in his life.

Miss W.

This woman of about thirty informed me that she had been troubled since her adolescent years by the urge to look compulsively at women and girls and that she was haunted by various erotic fantasies regarding her own sex. All of this was against her liking, and it was never her intention ever to accept it as normal. This sexual symptom appeared an expression of an inferiority complex that undermined her emotional life on every side. She was anxious in company, thought that others watched her contemptuously, and was often depressed; she could at times react furiously and rebelliously. Concerning her childhood, which had been marked by problems and worries in the family, I only want to point to the unfavorable influence of the lack of understanding she had felt on the part of her mother and to the destructive and distrustful remarks her father used to make.

As early as elementary school, she felt ridiculous and inferior to the other girls in almost every respect: clothes, way of speaking, physical appearance, and home situation. For years, she carried with her unresolved hurt—self-pity—about her unhappy fate; this went along with a generalized attitude of protest. In adolescence, this had been fertile ground for her admiration of other women and her yearning for intimate friendships.

One theme was central during her improvement process: becoming less of a pessimist. That implied that she should allow herself to be ruled less by self-critical ideas of her ugliness, worthlessness, and incapacities, by the expectation of becoming the victim of all kinds of misfortune, and by her overall complaining attitude that she was "born for misery." She was a classic example of a complainer, and although she conceded this, she remained inwardly convinced that she had a right to complain. With the help of her good will, she muddled through her severest depressions, combated her chronic complaining and rebelliousness, and as a result her general moods improved. The lesbian fantasies bothered her for some more years, but eventually they faded away. She tried to accept the feminine role and at times found herself reasonably successful as a woman. As to her feelings for men, these had never been completely absent, although they had not been central in her emotionality. For a while she engaged in a relationship with a man of about her own age, but in spite of her affection for him and of her being erotically interested in him, there were too many problems between them, and it seemed wiser to put an end to it. She could accept her situation of being alone after a short crisis; at present, she has a normal desire to be married and to have children.

These were brief descriptions of a few "average" cases. I hope the reader will gather from them that many positive things can be accomplished, provided we have good will, sincerity, and perseverence. In some cases the process of change passes more swiftly or with a better outcome than in the cases examined. Some others are more disappointing and more troublesome. Advantageous social factors that we should not fail to mention include having encouraging friends and a favorable family situation; furthermore, having sound moral convictions and a deep and personal religious life helps immeasurably. Disadvantages are a weak character, being a perpetual doubter, or having low moral standards, and of course, being enslaved to homosexual satisfactions for a long time.

To my mind, one thing is obvious. A fatalistic stand on the changeability of the homosexual orientation is not justified.

ELEVEN

Prevention

T HE SLOGAN THAT HOMOSEXUALITY should be accepted sounds deceptively humane to many ears; some have even been brainwashed so completely as to swallow the foolishness that homosexual relationships should enjoy the same rights as normal marriage. Those who are so enthusiastic about homosexual life, however, turn a blind eye to the sorrow that often goes along with it. They seem indifferent to the plight of adolescents and young adults who run the risk of failing in a central field of life when a homosexual development brings them to a deadlock. They do not even think about preventing this, although, objectively, there is no reason to take an a priori fatalistic stance in that respect.

From our exposition, a thing or two can be deduced about prevention. The first and foremost persons who can avert this stunted growth in their children are of course the parents. They must set the example of a normal man-woman relationship. If their marriage is good and they succeed reasonably in creating an atmosphere of cheerfulness and togetherness, they considerably reduce the chances of the coming into being of any neurotic complex, including the homosexual kind.

As to child-rearing practices, the father as well as the mother need to keep in mind that they must treat a boy as a boy and a girl as a girl. That does not mean forcing them into "prescribed roles," but cooperating with a child's natural propensities and taking account of innate behavioral sex-differences.

The *primordial* preventive factor is the parents' *appreciation* of the boy *as a boy* and of the girl *as a girl.* The children should perceive this appreciation. As we have already shown, shortcomings in connection with this must be avoided.

The critical periods for developing manly or womanly self-confidence are adolescence and preadolescence. Not only the parents, but also other persons outside the family can exert a beneficial influence at that age. Sometimes, for instance, teachers may positively contribute to strengthening a healthy gender confidence. They may encourage and help a certain child cross certain thresholds. Think, for example, of the boy who is systematically behind with games and sports, who is an outsider in his peer group; consider the importance of personal understanding that a teacher or another adult can express in a conversation or otherwise to help the adolescent avoid the danger of giving in to self-dramatization.

There is also a preventive effect in *good* sex education. Adolescents with certain types of original inferiority complexes can experience a depressing shock when being taught by such an "enlightened" authority as a teacher that "homosexuality is inherent in the brain." Such nonsense nails a child to his self-doubts and can lead an undecided, undeveloped mind in a pernicious direction. Should the young person hear, on the other hand, that homosexual feelings in adolescence are a question of a developmental emotional problem, and that genuine, inborn homosexuality does not exist; moreover, that this orientation amounts to an inferiority complex that is susceptible to change—then the educator instills hope and points to a road on which inner growth can be resumed.

Notes

Chapter One
Current Social Attitudes toward Homosexuality

1. A.D. de Groot, "Hypothesen over homofilie," *De Psycholoog* 17 (1982), pp. 244-45.
2. An indication of this: in one study, 60 percent of "socially well-adapted" homosexuals (out of nearly 1000) had at some time applied for psychological or psychiatric help. See A.P. Bell, M.S. Weinberg, and S.K. Hammersmith, *Sexual Preference: Its Development in Men and Women* (Bloomington: Indiana University Press, 1981).

Chapter Two
When Is One a Homosexual?

1. E. Sbardelini and E.T. Sbardelini, "Homossexualismo masculino e homossexualismo feminino: Neuroticismo e fatores psicológicos na infância" (Unpublished research report; Campinas, São Paulo: Universidade Católica, Department of Psychology, 1977).
2. G. Sigmund, *Die Natur der menschlichen Sexualität* (Würzburg: J.W. Naumann, 1972).
3. The story of his painful but ultimately successful effort to free himself from his homosexual feelings is told in W. Aaron, *Straight: A Heterosexual Talks about His Homosexual Past* (New York: Doubleday, 1972).
4. D. Hanson, *Homosexuality: The International Disease* (New York: L.S. Publications, 1965)

Chapter Three
Is Homosexuality "Inherent?"

1. S. Meilof-Oonk, et al., *Homosexualiteit: Een onderzoek naar beeldvorming en attitude bij de meerderjarige Nederlandse bevolking* (Amsterdam: Stichting Bevordering Sociaal Onderzoek Minderheden, 1969)
2. "Sick Again?" *Time*, 20 February 1978.
3. A.P. Bell, M.S. Weinberg, and S.K. Hammersmith, *Sexual Preference: Its Development in Men and Women* (Bloomington: Indiana University Press, 1981).

4. M. Schofield, *Sociological Aspects of Homosexuality* (London: Longmans, Green, 1965).
5. W.H. Perloff, "Hormones and Homosexuality" in *Sexual Inversion*, ed. J. Marmor (New York: Basic Books, 1965).
6. R.C. Kolodny, et al. "Plasma Testosterone and Semen Analysis in Male Homosexuals," *New England Journal of Medicine* 285 (1971), pp. 1170-74.
7. R.B. Evans, "Physical and Biochemical Characteristics of Homosexual Men," *Journal of Consulting and Clinical Psychology* 39 (1972), pp. 140-47.
8. G.J.M. van den Aardweg and J. Bonda, *Een netelig vraagstuk: Homofilie, geloof en psychologie* (Nijkerk: Callenbach, 1981).
9. Evans, "Physical and Biochemical Characteristics."
10. J. Money and A.A. Ehrhardt, *Man and Woman, Boy and Girl: The Differentiation and Dimorphism of Gender Identity from Conception to Maturity* (Baltimore: Johns Hopkins University Press, 1972).
11. D.J. West, *Homosexuality* (London: Penguin Books, 1960).
12. F.J. Kallmann, "Comparative Twin Studies on the Genetic Aspects of Male Homosexuality," *Journal of Nervous and Mental Disease* 115 (1952), pp. 283-98.
13. J.D. Rainer et al., "Homosexuality and Heterosexuality in Identical Twins," *Psychosomatic Medicine* 22 (1960), pp. 251-59; R.C. Friedman et al., "Psychological Development and Blood Level of Sex Steroids in Male Identical Twins of Divergent Sexual Orientation," *Journal of Nervous and Mental Disease* 163 (1974), pp. 282-88.
14. Van den Aardweg and Bonda, *Een netelig vraagstuk.*
15. W.H. Masters and V.E. Johnson, *Homosexuality in Perspective* (Boston: Little, Brown and Company, 1979).
16. L.J. Hatterer, *Changing Homosexuality in the Male* (New York: McGraw-Hill, 1970).
17. G.J.M. van den Aardweg, *Homofilie, neurose en dwangzelfbeklag* (Amsterdam: Polak & Van Gennep, 1967).
18. Masters and Johnson, *Homosexuality in Perspective.*
19. I. Eibl Eibesfeld, *Liebe und Hass* (Munich: Piper, 1970).
20. A. Karlen, *Sexuality and Homosexuality* (New York: Norton, 1971).
21. R. Flacelière, *Amour en Grèce* (Paris: Hachette, 1960).
22. R.W. Goy and B.S. McEwen, *Sexual Differentiation of the Brain* (Cambridge, Mass.: MIT Press, 1980).
23. R. May, *Sex and Fantasy: Patterns of Male and Female Development* (New York: Norton, 1980).
24. Van den Aardweg and Bonda, *Een netelig vraagstuk*; Money and Ehrhardt, *Man and Woman.*

Chapter Four
Homosexuality as a Psychological Disturbance

1. Alfred Adler, *Das Problem der Homosexualität* (Munich: Reinhardt, 1917).

2. W. Stekel, *Onanie und Homosexualität* (Vienna: Urban & Schwarzenberg, 1921).
3. W. Stekel, *Psychosexueller Infantilismus* (Vienna: Urban & Schwarzenberg, 1922).
4. E. Bergler, *Homosexuality: Disease or Way of Life?* (New York: Hill & Wang, 1957).
5. I. Bieber et al., *Homosexuality: A Psychoanalytic Study* (New York: Basic Books, 1962).
6. Some studies reporting these factors include R.B. Evans, "Childhood Parental Relationships of Homosexual Men," *Journal of Consulting and Clinical Psychology* 33 (1969), pp. 129-35; J.R. Snortum et al., "Family Dynamics and Homosexuality," *Psychological Reports* 24 (1969), pp. 763-70; N.L. Thomson et al., "Parent-Child Relationships and Sexual Identity in Male and Female Homosexuals and Heterosexuals," *Journal of Consulting and Clinical Psychology* 41 (1975), pp. 120-27; W.G. Stephan, "Parental Relationships and Early Social Experiences of Activist Male Homosexuals and Male Heterosexuals," *Journal of Abnormal Psychology* 82 (1973), pp. 506-13; M. Siegelman, "Parental Backgrounds of Male Homosexuals and Heterosexuals," *Archives of Sexual Behavior* 3 (1974), pp. 3-18; and G.J.M. van den Aardweg, "De faktor 'klaagziekte,' neurose en homofilie," *Psychologica Belgica* 13 (1973), pp. 295-311.
7. Stekel, *Onanie und Homosexualität*.
8. J.L. Arndt, *Zelfdramatisiering* (Leiden: Stenfert Kroese, 1950).
9. J.L. Arndt, "Een bijdrage tot het inzicht in de homosexualiteit," *Geneeskundige Bladen* 3 (1961), pp. 65-105.
10. P. Madison, *Freud's Concept of Repression and Defense* (Minneapolis: University of Minnesota Press, 1961).
11. J. Breuer and Sigmund Freud, *Studien über Hysterie* (Vienna: Deuticke, 1895).
12. G.J.M. van den Aardweg, "A Grief Theory of Homosexuality," *American Journal of Psychotherapy* 26 (1972), pp. 52-68.
13. D.S. Holmes, "Investigations of Repression," *Psychological Bulletin* 81 (1974), pp. 632-53.
14. Karen Horney, *Our Inner Conflicts* (New York: Norton, 1975).
15. Harry Stack Sullivan, *The Interpersonal Theory of Psychiatry* (New York: Norton, 1953).
16. M. Eck, *Sodome: Essai sur l'homosexualité* (Paris: Anthème Fayard, 1966).
17. Charles W. Socarides, *The Overt Homosexual* (New York: Grune and Stratton, 1968); idem, *Homosexuality* (New York: Aronson, 1978).
18. L.J. Hatterer, *Changing Homosexuality in the Male* (New York: McGraw-Hill, 1970).
19. On attempts to establish such a test, see H.J. Eysenck, *The Scientific Study of Personality* (London: Routledge & Kegan Paul, 1952); idem, *The Dynamics of Anxiety and Hysteria* (London: Routledge & Kegan Paul, 1957); idem, *Experiments in Personality*, 2 vols. (London: Routledge & Kegan Paul, 1960); H.J. Eysenck, G.W. Granger, and J.C. Brengelmann, *Perceptual Processes and Mental Illness* (London: Chapman and Hall,

122 / *Homosexuality and Hope*

1957); R.B. Cattell, *Personality and Motivation Structure and Measurement* (New York: World Book Company, 1957); R.B. Cattell and I.H. Scheier, *The Meaning and Measurement of Neuroticism and Anxiety* (New York: Ronald Press, 1961). One possible candidate for such a test, H.J. Eysenck, *Dimensions in Personality* (London: Routledge & Kegan Paul, 1947), proved to be a failure on replication: G. Claridge, "The Excitation-Inhibition Balance in Neurotics," in *Experiments in Personality*, ed. H.J. Eysenck, vol. 2 (London: Routledge & Kegan Paul, 1960).

20. Eysenck, *Scientific Study of Personality*.
21. Many questionnaires of this type exist, usually called "neuroticism" questionnaires: several scales or subquestionnaires of the Minnesota Multiple Personality Inventory (MMPI) (W.G. Dahlstrom and G.S. Welsh, *An MMPI Handbook* (St. Paul: North Publishing Company, 1960)); the MAS (J.A. Taylor, "A Personality Scale of Manifest Anxiety," *Journal of Abnormal and Social Psychology* 48 (1953), pp. 285-90); the Cornell Medical Index (K. Brodman, A.J. Erdman, I. Lorge, C.P. Gerhenson, and H.G. Wolff, "The Cornell Medical Index Health Questionnaire III: The Evaluation of Emotional Disturbance," *Journal of Clinical Psychology* 8 (1952), pp. 119-24); some scales of the Sixteen Personality Factor Test (16 PF) (R.B. Cattell and G.F. Stice, *Handbook of the Sixteen Personality Factor Questionnaire* (Champaign, Illinois: Institute for Personality and Ability Testing, 1957)); of the Maudsley Personality Inventory (MPI) (H.J. Eysenck, *Manual of the Maudsley Personality Inventory* (London: University of London Press, 1959)); and of the Eysenck Personality Inventory (EPI) (H.J. Eysenck and S.B.G. Eysenck, *Manual of the Eysenck Personality Inventory* (London: University of London Press, 1964)). They have been given different names, but factor-analytic studies have made it clear that all of them are so highly correlated that they may be rightly thought of as being more or less identical, measuring the same general factor of "neuroticism" or "neurotic emotionality." A.W. Bendig, "Factor Analyses of 'Anxiety' and 'Neuroticism' Inventories," *Journal of Consulting Psychology* 24 (1960), pp. 161-68; H.J. Eysenck and S.B.G. Eysenck, *Personality Structure and Measurement* (London: Routledge & Kegan Paul, 1969); and J.P. Guilford, "Factors and Factors of Personality," *Psychological Bulletin* 82 (1975), pp. 802-14.
22. Tests confirming this finding have used the MMPI, the 16 PF, the MPI, the EPI, the Neuroticism Scale Questionnaire (NSQ), and the Maudsley Medical Questionnaire (MMQ). Studies involving clinical groups of homosexuals (those already in treatment) are: G.J.M. van den Aardweg, *Homofilie, neurose en dwangzelfbeklag* (Amsterdam: Polak & Van Gennep, 1967) (Holland, MMPI and MPI); W.A. Oliver and D.L. Mosher, "Psychopathology and Guilt in Heterosexual and Subgroups of Homosexual Reformatory Inmates," *Journal of Abnormal Psychology* 73 (1968), pp. 323-29 (U.S., MMPI); R.B. Cattell and J.H. Morony, "The Use of 16 PF in Distinguishing Homosexuals, Normals, and

General Criminals," *Journal of Consulting Psychology* 26 (1952), pp. 531-40 (Australia, 16 PF); A.W. Vermeul-van Mullem, "Het voorkomen van de zogenaamde homosexuele signs in de Rorschachtest" (Unpublished research report; Amsterdam: Gemeente Universiteit, Department of Psychology, 1960) (Holland, MMQ); and M.P. Feldman and M.J. MacCulloch, *Homosexual Behaviour, Therapy and Assessment* (Oxford: Pergamon Press, 1971) (Britain, 16 PF and EPI). Those using nonclinical groups of homosexuals are Cattell and Morony, "Use of the 16 PF"; W.T. Doidge and W.H. Holtzman, "Implications of Homosexuality among Air Force Trainees," *Journal of Consulting Psychology* 24 (1960), pp. 9-13 (U.S., MMPI); R.B. Dean and H. Richardson, "Analysis of MMPI Profiles of Forty College-educated Overt Male Homosexuals," *Journal of Consulting Psychology* 28 (1964), pp. 483-86 (U.S., MMPI); L.J. Braaten and C.D. Darling, "Overt and Covert Homosexual Problems among Male College Students," *Genetic Psychology Monographs* 71 (1965), pp. 269-310 (U.S., MMPI); M. Manosevitz, "Early Sexual Behavior in Adult Homosexual and Heterosexual Males," *Journal of Abnormal Psychology* 76 (1970), pp. 396-402 (U.S., MMPI); idem, "Education and MMPI-Mf Scores in Homosexual and Heterosexual Males," *Journal of Consulting and Clinical Psychology* 36 (1971), pp. 395-99 (U.S., MMPI); R.B. Evans, "Sixteen Personality Factor Questionnaire Scores of Homosexual Men," *Journal of Consulting and Clinical Psychology* 34 (1970), pp. 212-15 (U.S., 16 PF); M. Siegelman, "Adjustment of Male Homosexuals and Heterosexuals," *Archives of Sexual Behavior* 2 (1972), pp. 9-25 (U.S., NSQ); idem, "Psychological Adjustment of Homosexual and Heterosexual Men: A Cross-national Replication," *Archives of Sexual Behavior* 7 (1978), pp. 1-11 (Britain, NSQ); H.P. Liong A Kong, "Neurotische labiliteit en homofilie bij mannen" (Unpublished research report; Amsterdam: Vrije Universiteit, Department of Psychology, 1965) (Holland, MPI); and E. Sbardelini and E.T. Sbardelini, "Homossexualismo masculino e homossexualismo feminino: Neuroticismo e fatores psicológicos na infância" (Unpublished research report; Campinas, São Paulo: Universidade Católica, Department of Psychology, 1977).

Chapter Five
The Homosexual Inferiority Complex

1. J.L. Arndt, *Genese en psychotherapie der neurose,* 2 vols. (The Hague: Boucher, 1962).
2. E. Bergler, *Counterfeit Sex* (New York: Grune & Stratton, 1958).
3. S. Goldberg, *The Inevitability of Patriarchy* (London: Temple Smith, 1977).
4. R. May, *Sex and Fantasy: Patterns of Male and Female Development* (New York: Norton, 1980).
5. M. Dannecker, *Der Homosexuelle und die Homosexualität* (Frankfurt: Syndikat, 1978).

Chapter Six
Origin and Functioning of the Homosexual Complex

1. Many studies have confirmed this pattern. See I. Bieber et al., *Homosexuality: A Psychoanalytic Study* (New York: Basic Books, 1962); R.B. Evans, "Childhood Parental Relationships of Homosexual Men," *Journal of Consulting and Clinical Psychology* 33 (1969), pp. 129-35; J.R. Snortum et al., "Family Dynamics and Homosexuality," *Psychological Reports* 24 (1969), pp. 763-70; N.L. Thomson et al., "Parent-Child Relationships and Sexual Identity in Male and Female Homosexuals and Heterosexuals," *Journal of Consulting and Clinical Psychology* 41 (1975), pp. 120-27; W.G. Stephan, "Parental Relationships and Early Social Experiences of Activist Male Homosexuals and Male Heterosexuals," *Journal of Abnormal Psychology* 82 (1973), pp. 506-13; M. Siegelman, "Parental Backgrounds of Male Homosexuals and Heterosexuals," *Archives of Sexual Behavior* 3 (1974), pp. 3-18; G.J.M. van den Aardweg, "De faktor 'klaagziekte,' neurose en homofilie," *Psychologica Belgica* 13 (1973), pp. 295-311.

2. The author has discussed this question at greater length in G.J.M. van den Aardweg, "Parents of Homosexuals: Not Guilty?" *American Journal of Psychotherapy* 38 (1984), pp. 180-89.

3. I. Bieber and T. Bieber, "Male Homosexuality," *Canadian Journal of Psychiatry* 24 (1979), pp. 409-22.

4. G.J.M. van den Aardweg, "De neurose van Couperus," *Nederlands Tijdschrift voor de Psychologie* 20 (1965), pp. 293-307.

5. Bieber et al., *Homosexuality*; Evans, "Childhood Parental Relationships"; Thomson et al., "Parent-Child Relationships and Sexual Identity"; Stephan, "Parental Relationships"; E. Sbardelini and E.T. Sbardelini, "Homossexualismo masculino e homossexualismo feminino: Neuroticismo e fatores psicologicos na infância" (Unpublished research report; Campinas, São Paulo: Universidade Católica, Department of Psychology, 1977).

6. It has been argued that shortcomings like the ones described in parent-child relationships of homosexually oriented persons occur only with those who land in the consulting room of the psychologist and the psychiatrist. That is incorrect. As in the case of personality tests (see above, chapter 4, nn. 19-22), statistics and observations on this subject have been collected in all kinds of groups, including samples of homosexuals who are socially well-adapted and functioning.

7. Some studies on this topic include: E. Bene, "On the Genesis of Female Homosexuality," *British Journal of Psychiatry* 111 (1965), pp. 815-21; E. Kaye et al., "Homosexuality in Women," *Archives of General Psychiatry* 17 (1967), pp. 626-34; F.E. Kenyon, "Studies in Female Homosexuality: Psychological Test Results," *Journal of Consulting and Clinical Psychology* 32 (1968), pp. 510-13; M.W. Kremer and A.H. Rifkin, "Early Development of Homosexuality: A Study of Adolescent Lesbians," *American*

Journal of Psychiatry 126 (1969), pp. 91-96; R.H. Gundlach and B.F. Riess, "Self and Sexual Identity in the Female: A Study of Female Homosexuals," in *New Directions in Mental Health*, ed. B.F. Riess (New York: Grune & Stratton, 1968); and D.W. Swanson et al., "Clinical Features of the Female Homosexual Patient: A Comparison with the Heterosexual Patient," *Journal of Nervous and Mental Disease* 155 (1972), pp. 119-24.
8. Gundlach and Riess, "Self and Sexual Identity."

Chapter Nine
Change without Psychotherapy

1. W.J. Sengers, *Homoseksualiteit als klacht: Een psychiatrische studie* (Bussum: Paul Brand, 1969).
2. The religious reorientation of life is sometimes methodically pursued, e.g., by the Jesuit method of "discernment of spirits" (which "spirit" or mental attitude is the right one, the one desired by God, and which is the wrong one we should avoid?). Application of this method sometimes cures a homosexual "as a side-effect," as the Dutch Catholic priest and publicist Dr. Penning de Vries has communicated to me. However, the primary goal of this method is not primarily to cure a neurosis, but to reorient a person's life according to biblical principles.
3. J.T. Bos, *Ik ben niet meer "zo"* (Hoornaar: Gideon, 1969).
4. Though remaining deeply religious, the man's exaltation has sobered down a great deal since that time. He himself is inclined to see his change now as a psychic struggle, motivated and greatly encouraged by his religious conversion, prayer, and overall change of way of life.
5. L.J. Hatterer, *Changing Homosexuality in the Male* (New York: McGraw-Hill, 1970).

Chapter Ten
Effects of Anticomplaining Therapy

1. G.J.M. van den Aardweg, *On the Origins and Therapy of Homosexuality: A Psychoanalytic Re-interpretation* (New York: Praeger, in press).

Bibliography

Aaron, W. *Straight: A Heterosexual Talks about His Homosexual Past.* New York: Doubleday, 1972.

Adler, Alfred. *Das Problem der Homosexualität.* Munich: Reinhardt, 1917.

Arndt, J.L. "Een bijdrage tot het inzicht in de homosexualiteit." *Geneeskundige Bladen* 3 (1961), pp. 65-105.

Arndt, J.L. *Genese en psychotherapie der neurose.* 2 vols. The Hague: Boucher, 1962.

Arndt, J.L. *Zelfdramatisiering.* Leiden: Stenfert Kroese, 1950.

Bell, A.P.; Weinberg, M.S.; and Hammersmith, S.K., *Sexual Preference: Its Development in Men and Women.* Bloomington: Indiana University Press, 1981.

Bendig, A.W. "Factor Analyses of 'Anxiety' and 'Neuroticism' Inventories." *Journal of Consulting Psychology* 24 (1960), pp. 161-68.

Bene, E. "On the Genesis of Female Homosexuality." *British Journal of Psychiatry* 111 (1965), pp. 815-21.

Bergler, E. *Counterfeit Sex.* New York: Grune & Stratton, 1958.

Bergler, E. *Homosexuality: Disease or Way of Life?* New York: Hill & Wang, 1957.

Bieber, I., and Bieber, T. "Male Homosexuality." *Canadian Journal of Psychiatry* 24 (1979), pp. 409-22.

Bieber, I., et al. *Homosexuality: A Psychoanalytic Study.* New York: Basic Books, 1962.

Bos, J.T. *Ik ben niet meer "zo."* Hoornaar: Gideon, 1969.

Braaten, L.J., and Darling, C.D. "Overt and Covert Homosexual Problems among Male College Students." *Genetic Psychology Monographs* 71 (1965), pp. 269-310.

Breuer, J., and Freud, Sigmund. *Studien über Hysterie.* Vienna: Deuticke, 1895.

Brodman, K.; Erdman, A.J.; Lorge, I.; Gerhenson, C.P.; and Wolff, H.G., "The Cornell Medical Index Health Questionnaire III: The Evaluation of Emotional Disturbance." *Journal of Clinical Psychology* 8 (1952), pp. 119-24.

Cattell, R.B. *Personality and Motivation Structure and Measurement.* New York: World Book Company, 1957.

Cattell, R.B., and Morony, J.H. "The Use of 16 PF in Distinguishing Homosexuals, Normals, and General Criminals." *Journal of Consulting Psychology* 26 (1952), pp. 531-40.

Cattell, R.B., and Scheier, I.H. *The Meaning and Measurement of Neuroticism and Anxiety.* New York: Ronald Press, 1961.

Cattell, R.B., and Stice, G.F. *Handbook of the Sixteen Personality Factor Questionnaire.* Champaign, Illinois: Institute for Personality and Ability Testing, 1957.

Claridge, G. "The Excitation-Inhibition Balance in Neurotics." In *Experiments in Personality,* edited by H.J. Eysenck, vol. 2. London: Routledge & Kegan Paul, 1960.

Dahlstrom, W.G., and Welsh, G.S. *An MMPI Handbook.* St. Paul: North Publishing Company, 1960.

Dannecker, M. *Der Homosexuelle und die Homosexualität.* Frankfurt: Syndikat, 1978.

De Groot, A.D. "Hypothesen over homofilie." *De Psycholoog* 17 (1982), pp. 244-45.

Dean, R.B., and Richardson, H. "Analysis of MMPI Profiles of Forty College-educated Overt Male Homosexuals." *Journal of Consulting Psychology* 28 (1964), pp. 483-86.

Doidge, W.T., and Holtzman, W.H. "Implications of Homosexuality among Air Force Trainees." *Journal of Consulting Psychology* 24 (1960), pp. 9-13.

Eck, M. *Sodome: Essai sur l'homosexualité.* Paris: Anthème Fayard, 1966.

Eibl Eibesfeld, I. *Liebe und Hass.* Munich: Piper, 1970.

Evans, R.B. "Childhood Parental Relationships of Homosexual Men." *Journal of Consulting and Clinical Psychology* 33 (1969), pp. 129-35.

Evans, R.B. "Physical and Biochemical Characteristics of Homosexual Men." *Journal of Consulting and Clinical Psychology* 39 (1972), pp. 140-47.

Evans, R.B. "Sixteen Personality Factor Questionnaire Scores of

Homosexual Men." *Journal of Consulting and Clinical Psychology* 34 (1970), pp. 212-15.

Eysenck, H.J. *Dimensions in Personality.* London: Routledge and Kegan Paul, 1947.

Eysenck, H.J. *The Dynamics of Anxiety and Hysteria.* London: Routledge and Kegan Paul, 1957.

Eysenck, H.J. *Experiments in Personality.* 2 vols. London: Routledge and Kegan Paul, 1960.

Eysenck, H.J. *Manual of the Maudsley Personality Inventory.* London: University of London Press, 1959.

Eysenck, H.J. *The Scientific Study of Personality.* London: Routledge and Kegan Paul, 1952.

Eysenck, H.J., and Eysenck, S.B.G. *Manual of the Eysenck Personality Inventory.* London: University of London Press, 1964.

Eysenck, H.J., and Eysenck, S.B.G. *Personality Structure and Measurement.* London: Routledge and Kegan Paul, 1969.

Eysenck, H.J.; Granger, G.W.; and Brengelmann, J.C. *Perceptual Processes and Mental Illness.* London: Chapman and Hall, 1957.

Feldman, M.P., and MacCulloch, M.J. *Homosexual Behaviour, Therapy and Assessment.* Oxford: Pergamon Press, 1971.

Flacelière, R. *Amour en Grèce.* Paris: Hachette, 1960.

Freedman, M. "Homosexuality among Women and Psychological Adjustment." Ph.D. diss., Western Reserve University, 1967.

Freedman, M. *Homosexuality and Psychological Functioning.* Belmont: Brooks & Cole Publishing Company, 1971.

Friedman, R.C., et al. "Psychological Development and Blood Level of Sex Steroids in Male Identical Twins of Divergent Sexual Orientation." *Journal of Nervous and Mental Disease* 163 (1974), pp. 282-88.

Goldberg, S. *The Inevitability of Patriarchy.* London: Temple Smith, 1977.

Goy, R.W., and McEwen, B.S. *Sexual Differentiation of the Brain.* Cambridge, Mass.: MIT Press, 1980.

Guilford, J.P. "Factors and Factors of Personality." *Psychological Bulletin* 82 (1975), pp. 802-14.

Gundlach, R.H., and Riess, B.F. "Self and Sexual Identity in the Female: A Study of Female Homosexuals." In *New Directions in Mental Health,* edited by B.F. Riess. New York: Grune & Stratton, 1968.

Hanson, D. *Homosexuality: The International Disease.* New York: L.S. Publications, 1965.

Hatterer, L.J. *Changing Homosexuality in the Male.* New York: McGraw-Hill, 1970.

Holmes, D.S. "Investigations of Repression." *Psychological Bulletin* 81 (1974), pp. 632-53.

Hopkins, J.H. "The Lesbian Personality." *British Journal of Psychiatry* 115 (1969), pp. 1433-36.

Horney, Karen. *Our Inner Conflicts.* New York: Norton, 1975.

Kallmann, F.J. "Comparative Twin Studies on the Genetic Aspects of Male Homosexuality." *Journal of Nervous and Mental Disease* 115 (1952), pp. 283-98.

Karlen, A. *Sexuality and Homosexuality.* New York: Norton, 1971.

Kaye, E., et al. "Homosexuality in Women." *Archives of General Psychiatry* 17 (1967), pp. 626-34.

Kenyon, F.E. "Studies in Female Homosexuality: Psychological Test Results." *Journal of Consulting and Clinical Psychology* 32 (1968), pp. 510-13.

Kolodny, R.C., et al. "Plasma Testosterone and Semen Analysis in Male Homosexuals." *New England Journal of Medicine* 285 (1971), pp. 1170-74.

Kremer, M.W., and Rifkin, A.H. "Early Development of Homosexuality: A Study of Adolescent Lesbians." *American Journal of Psychiatry* 126 (1969), pp. 91-96.

Liong A Kong, H.P. "Neurotische labiliteit en homofilie bij mannen." Unpublished research report; Amsterdam: Vrije Universiteit, Department of Psychology, 1965.

Madison, P. *Freud's Concept of Repression and Defense.* Minneapolis: University of Minnesota Press, 1961.

Manosevitz, M. "Early Sexual Behavior in Adult Homosexual and Heterosexual Males." *Journal of Abnormal Psychology* 76 (1970), pp. 396-402.

Manosevitz, M. "Education and MMPI-Mf Scores in Homosexual and Heterosexual Males." *Journal of Consulting and Clinical Psychology* 36 (1971), pp. 395-99.

Masters, W.H., and Johnson, V.E. *Homosexuality in Perspective.* Boston: Little, Brown and Company, 1979.

May, R. *Sex and Fantasy: Patterns of Male and Female Development.* New York: Norton, 1980.

Meilof-Oonk, S., et al. *Homosexualiteit: Een onderzoek naar beeld-vorming en attitude bij de meerdejarige Nederlandse bevolking.* Amsterdam: Stichting Bevordering Sociaal Onderzoek Minderheden, 1969.

Money, J., and Ehrhardt, A.A. *Man and Woman, Boy and Girl: The Differentiation and Dimorphism of Gender Identity from Conception to Maturity.* Baltimore: Johns Hopkins University Press, 1972.

Oliver, W.A., and Mosher, D.L. "Psychopathology and Guilt in Heterosexual and Subgroups of Homosexual Reformatory Inmates." *Journal of Abnormal Psychology* 73 (1968), pp. 323-29.

Perloff, W.H. "Hormones and Homosexuality." In *Sexual Inversion,* edited by J. Marmor. New York: Basic Books, 1965.

Rainer, J.D., et al. "Homosexuality and Heterosexuality in Identical Twins." *Psychosomatic Medicine* 22 (1960), pp. 251-59.

Sbardelini, E. and Sbardelini, E.T. "Homossexualismo masculino e homossexualismo feminino: Neuroticismo e fatores psicológicos na infância." Unpublished research report; Campinas, São Paulo: Universidade Católica, Department of Psychology, 1977.

Schofield, M. *Sociological Aspects of Homosexuality.* London: Longmans, Green and Co., 1965.

Sengers, W.J. *Homoseksualiteit als klacht: Een psychiatrische studie.* Bussum: Paul Brand, 1969.

"Sick Again?" *Time,* 20 February 1978.

Siegelman, M. "Adjustment of Male Homosexuals and Heterosexuals." *Archives of Sexual Behavior* 2 (1972), pp. 9-25.

Siegelman, M. "Parental Backgrounds of Male Homosexuals and Heterosexuals." *Archives of Sexual Behavior* 3 (1974), pp. 3-18.

Siegelman, M. "Psychological Adjustment of Homosexual and Heterosexual Men: A Cross-national Replication." *Archives of Sexual Behavior* 7 (1978), pp. 1-11.

Sigmund, G. *Die Natur der menschlichen Sexualität.* Würzburg: J.W. Naumann, 1972.

Snortum, J.R., et al. "Family Dynamics and Homosexuality." *Psychological Reports* 24 (1969), pp. 763-70.

Socarides, Charles W. *Homosexuality.* New York: Aronson, 1978.

Socarides, Charles W. *The Overt Homosexual.* New York: Grune and Stratton, 1968.

Stekel, W. *Onanie und Homosexualität.* Vienna: Urban & Schwarzenberg, 1921.

Stekel, W. *Psychosexueller Infantilismus.* Vienna: Urban & Schwarzenberg, 1922.

Stephan, W.G. "Parental Relationships and Early Social Experiences of Activist Male Homosexuals and Male Heterosexuals." *Journal of Abnormal Psychology* 82 (1973), pp. 506-13.

Sullivan, Harry Stack. *The Interpersonal Theory of Psychiatry.* New York: Norton, 1953.

Swanson, D.W., et al. "Clinical Features of the Female Homosexual Patient: A Comparison with the Heterosexual Patient." *Journal of Nervous and Mental Disease* 155 (1972), pp. 119-24.

Taylor, J.A. "A Personality Scale of Manifest Anxiety." *Journal of Abnormal and Social Psychology* 48 (1953), pp. 285-90.

Thomson, N.L., et al. "Parent-Child Relationships and Sexual Identity in Male and Female Homosexuals and Heterosexuals." *Journal of Consulting and Clinical Psychology* 41 (1975), pp. 120-27.

Van den Aardweg, G.J.M. "De faktor 'klaagziekte,' neurose en homofilie." *Psychologica Belgica* 13 (1973), pp. 295-311.

Van den Aardweg, G.J.M. "A Grief Theory of Homosexuality." *American Journal of Psychotherapy* 26 (1972), pp. 52-68.

Van den Aardweg, G.J.M. *Homofilie, neurose en dwangzelfbeklag.* Amsterdam: Polak & Van Gennep, 1967.

Van den Aardweg, G.J.M. "De neurose van Couperus." *Nederlands Tijdschrift voor de Psychologie* 20 (1965), pp. 293-307.

Van den Aardweg, G.J.M. "Parents of Homosexuals: Not Guilty?" *American Journal of Psychotheraphy* 38 (1984), pp. 180-89.

Van den Aardweg, G.J.M. *On the Origins and Therapy of Homosexuality: A Psychoanalytic Re-interpretation.* New York: Praeger, in press.

Van den Aardweg, G.J.M., and Bonda, J. *Een netelig vraagstuk: Homofilie, geloof en psychologie.* Nijkerk: Callenbach, 1981.

Vermeul-van Mullem, A.W. "Het voorkomen van de zogenaamde homosexuele signs in de Rorschachtest." Unpublished research report; Amsterdam: Gemeente Universiteit, Department of Psychology, 1960.

West, D.J. *Homosexuality.* London: Penguin Books, 1960.

Index